Praise for *Travels Through Middle Earth*

"This book is a thorough and enjoyable voyage into the heart of modern Anglo-Saxon spirituality. With his breezy style and quick wit, the author displays a practical approach to this religion that is both fascinating and informative. I heartily recommend this book to everyone, particularly folks new to this path!"

—Rev. Kirk S. Thomas, ADF Vice-Archdruid

D1251505

Travels Through
middle earth

About the Author

Alaric Albertsson began his spiritual journey when he was introduced to the Anglo-Saxon gods and goddesses in 1971. Over the past four decades, his personal spiritual practice has developed as a synthesis of Anglo-Saxon tradition, country folklore, herbal studies, and rune lore. A native of Missouri and Arkansas, Alaric now resides in western Pennsylvania where he is a founding member of Earendel Hearth, an Anglo-Saxon *inhíred*. For more information, visit www.alaricalbertsson.com.

travels through
middle earth

the path of
a saxon pagan

ALARIC ALBERTSSON

Llewellyn Publications
Woodbury, Minnesota

First Edition
First Printing, 2009

Cover art: Antlers © iStockphoto and the chalice © PhotoDisc
Cover design by Kevin R. Brown
Llewellyn is a registered trademark of Llewellyn Worldwide, Ltd.

Library of Congress Cataloging-in-Publication Data
Albertsson, Alaric.
  Travels through middle earth : the path of a Saxon pagan / Alaric Albertsson.—1st ed.
      p. cm.
  Includes bibliographical references (p.   ).
  ISBN 978-0-7387-1536-0
  1. Anglo-Saxons—Religion. 2. Civilization, Anglo-Saxon. 3. Paganism—England—History. I. Title.
  BL980.G7A43 2009
  299'.94—dc22

                                                                    2009008297

Llewellyn Publications
A Division of Llewellyn Worldwide, Ltd.
2143 Wooddale Drive, Dept. 978-0-7387-1536-0
Woodbury, Minnesota 55125-2989, U.S.A.
www.llewellyn.com

Printed in the United States of America

Contents

Introduction

It was almost exactly one year ago today when my friend Christopher Penczak suggested that I write a book on Anglo-Saxon spirituality. Christopher, of course, is himself a prolific author, so I didn't dismiss the idea. The question, for me, was how to approach the subject. You see, contemporary Anglo-Saxon religious practices vary enormously from one group to another, from one person to another. The old gods are alive and have been inspiring men and women to reconstruct the *fyrn sidu*, the elder customs, for decades now. How could I encompass everyone's ideas and practices? Could I fairly represent Anglo-Saxon organizations that I've never belonged to, such as the various Theodish groups? Was it possible to write a book that would include all of the people who practice some form of Anglo-Saxon Heathenry today?

Ultimately I decided to focus on my own specific path. That's why this book is subtitled "The Path of a Saxon

Pagan" instead of "The Path of *the* Saxon Pagan." I don't pretend to speak for everyone. I speak only for myself, and for those who follow a path similar to mine. Of course, it's quite likely that many readers will eventually be drawn to Anglo-Saxon groups with practices and beliefs that are wildly different from what I describe in this book. I leave that to my gods. I don't claim that my way is better than any other.

The decision to focus on my own path evolved as I began to visualize the audience I was hoping to reach. This book has been written for the person who is seeking a path to spiritual fulfillment. Within these pages, you will be introduced to Anglo-Saxon beliefs, and to a spiritual practice that has evolved with me over the past thirty-seven years. It is not something I developed in a vacuum, of course. Over the years, countless men and women, directly or indirectly, have influenced how I approach the gods and spirits. The first polytheists I met in the early 1970s revered gods with names like Woden and Hertha, but their focus leaned heavily toward witchcraft. In retrospect I can see how deeply they were inspired by authors such as Paul Huson and Louise Huebner. Of course spellcasting—*wiccecræft*— is a venerable Anglo-Saxon institution, but it is far from the entirety of the elder customs. I'm sure these earliest experiences have had some influence on me on multiple levels.

At that time, the parents of one of my best friends were Spiritualists, and that, too, had a considerable influence on me. It wasn't unusual for me to join them for séances in their home. Because of these experiences, I've never perceived "spirit" as something abstract. For me, conversing with a spirit is no more extraordinary than calling a friend on the phone. Which, if you think about it, is something of a miracle in itself.

It wasn't long before I encountered the Wiccan religion, which at that time existed only as an initiatory tradition. The rituals were long and formulaic. To this day, I strongly prefer that words spoken during a ritual be spoken from the heart, rather than read or recited by rote.

Then, as now, Wicca was largely eclectic, and I might have drifted away from the Anglo-Saxon gods completely had it not been for the publication of Ray Buckland's *The Tree: The Complete Book of Saxon Witchcraft* in 1974. This book espoused the worship of Woden and Freya (Fréo) and broke from Wicca's initiatory tradition by popularizing the idea of "self-dedication." From a Pagan perspective, *The Tree* was arguably one of the most important books of that decade. But it was nevertheless a book about Wicca, not about Anglo-Saxon religion. The Saxon deities and symbols were imagery draped over the duotheistic concepts formulated by Gerald Brosseau Gardner earlier in the century. Ultimately it wasn't what I was looking for.

I read what I could of the gods and goddesses of northern Europe and tried to synthesize this with my personal spiritual experiences. I traveled repeatedly to England to experience firsthand the environment where these gods were once revered. I visited ancient holy sites, such as Arbor Low and the Rollright Stones. Back here in the United States, at solstice and equinox, I left food offerings for the elves, often burying the offerings or hanging them from tree limbs.

Eventually I met other men and women who were reconstructing the elder customs, often in ways quite different from my own. Since then I've been influenced by the writings of Anglo-Saxon adherents such as Swain Wódening and Winifred Hodge, as well as personal interactions with other people who honor the old, northern gods. People like Ann Groa Sheffield, of the Medoburg kindred, Patricia Lafayllve, Steerswoman of the Troth, and Maria Stoy, who assists in facilitating the excellent Dedicant Program offered by Ár nDraíocht Féin. Although we don't always agree on how the gods should be approached and worshipped, the surprising thing is how much we have in common. Personal encounters with a deity or deities are often reported. There is a shared conviction that the gods are real, distinct persons, rather than static archetypes or Jungian constructs; a shared understanding that the tribe has intrinsic value, giving us the ability to be something greater than ourselves; a shared love of the myths and folklore and legends of England.

These commonalities are what I hope this book will convey to you, the reader. If you already identify as a Saxon Pagan, or as an Anglo-Saxon Heathen, or any other permutation of this concept, it's unlikely that you'll find anything completely surprising in the following chapters. Hopefully you may find some new perspective, even if you disagree with it.

We will begin the first chapter by looking at the Anglo-Saxon people, who they were, and how they perceived the cosmos. The second and third chapters continue on by introducing the Anglo-Saxon gods and, perhaps more importantly, how to approach them with reverence and respect. You will learn how to establish a *wéofod*, or altar, and how to select and present offerings that will be pleasing to the old gods. After this, we'll explore other spirits—elves and dwarves and ancestral spirits—and concepts such as honor and wyrd, which are so important to those of us who follow the elder customs.

There's even a chapter later on about magic, although I must emphasize here that magic is not essential to the old ways as described in this book. This is primarily a book about Saxon spirituality, about acknowledging and developing a relationship with the old gods. Spells and runes and charms have their place, of course, but this is not that place. We will look briefly at how the Anglo-Saxons perceived magic and then return to our focus on how to live and worship as a Saxon Pagan.

The chapter on mead making may seem out of place if you are unfamiliar with Anglo-Saxon culture. Mead is a fermented drink made from honey, and it was extremely important to the early English people. In religious rites today, it is often chosen as an offering for honoring the northern gods. Back in the 1970s, when commercially produced mead was almost impossible to find, I knew a lot of people who brewed their own. Now many liquor stores will carry at least one brand of mead. But mead making is surprisingly easy. We have a stronger connection with an offering that we've made ourselves, so why not give it a try?

The final chapters of the book describe how to establish your own *inhired* (Saxon household), celebrate the holy tides, and observe the life passages we all go through. As I mentioned, I believe it's important that we speak from the heart in our rites, so the ritual words that I give are minimal. They are not intended to be magical formulae, but rather guidelines to give you a general idea of what to say.

Before I bring this to a close, I need to thank all of Earendel—the members of my Saxon inhíred—who have been so helpful with their ideas and feedback. I need to thank Scott in particular for putting up with late dinners and long absences. Scott also helped me with the chapter on mead making, since he's so very good at it. My regret is that I can't share a sip of his brew with each of you. Of course, I need to thank Christopher Penczak, too, not only for putting the idea of writing a book into my head, but also for helping me along the way with tips and encouragement. And I would be remiss if I didn't give a nod to Elysia Gallo and Karl Anderson, of Llewellyn Worldwide, who gave me some wonderful suggestions that have improved the content of the book immensely.

Finally, I want to thank my dad, Albert, who through his own example has taught me the value of integrity and honor.

Writing this book has been a journey for me. I view it as an extension of the path I first began to tread nearly four decades ago. I hope that some of you, too, will come to appreciate this path and its wonder and mystery. May the gods favor us all as we continue along our travels through Middle Earth.

—Alaric Albertsson

Who Were the Anglo-Saxons?

On November 15, 655 CE, King Penda stood on the banks of the river Winwaed and prepared to lead his forces into what would be his final battle. Two of his allies had already deserted the field. Cadafael ap Cynfeddw of Gwynedd —who would hence be known as Cadomedd, the battle-shirker—fled with his troops the night before. Following this, the cowardly King Æðelwald of Deira retreated with his own men. The rushing waters of the Winwaed were impassable due to recent rains. Penda's army was severely weakened.

Still, the last of the great Pagan Saxon kings marched onward. Divine blood flowed through his veins. Penda, son of Pybba, was a descendant of none other than the god Woden himself, ten generations removed. He'd raised his kingdom of Mercia from an obscure region in Britain's midlands to one of the most formidable powers in the land. For half a century the English kings, one at a time, had been turning away from their old gods, but Penda of Mercia stayed faithful and true. He remained a defender of the customs and traditions of his ancestors. Being a polytheist, recognizing that his gods were not the only gods, Penda allowed his subjects to worship as they chose. And so many Mercians were Christians. However, King Penda was himself a proud Pagan king who followed the old ways.

Penda was a skillful and valorous warrior. Over the years he'd defeated many foes. But on that fateful November day in 655, King Penda of Mercia, descendant of Woden, was slain and decapitated by the forces of Northumbria.

Penda was the last of the Anglo-Saxons' Pagan kings. He was a great man. Even his enemies admitted his divine favor, attributing the credit for his victories to "diabolical agency." (During that era, Christian scribes routinely referred to all Pagan gods as "devils" or "diabolical.") Throughout his life, Penda truly was guided by his ancestor, Woden. But after Penda's death, his Pagan subjects were forced to convert, at least publicly, to the new religion of Christianity. The old religion was outlawed. Historians tell us that Penda's death also marked the death of the Pagan Saxon religion—the end of the old religion.

But as somebody else—somebody undoubtedly not a historian—once said, "It isn't over until the fat lady sings."

I am a Saxon Pagan. By this I mean that I revere the gods and spirits that were once honored by the Anglo-Saxon people. As it is for many other men and women today, my religion is a reconstruction or reinterpretation of the rites and traditions that King Penda held dear.

I describe myself as a Saxon Pagan, but I'm equally comfortable with labels such as Anglo-Saxon Pagan, Anglo-Saxon Heathen, or Saxon Heathen. The truth is, the people who we now know as the Anglo-Saxons had no name for their indigenous religion. If you could travel back through time to the fifth century and ask Saxon Pagans to name their beliefs and practices, the best they could do, perhaps, is describe them as the *fyrn sidu*, meaning the "elder customs" or "old ways." Fyrn Sidu, in fact, is another label used by some people today to describe my religion.

If all of this is confusing, it is because this path is a very new revival of a very old way of living, and most of us who follow this old path are still trying to establish some sense of identity. There are people today who call themselves Heathens but insist they aren't Pagan. However, both of these words originally described a rural person (*heathen* referring to a person who lived on the heath or moor). Rural people are traditionally conservative, and the rural folk of England remained true to their old ways after townspeople had abandoned their gods and converted to the new religion of Christianity. So these words describing the rural population—*pagan* and *heathen*—eventually came to mean people who were not Christians, Jews, or Muslims.

Admittedly, there are many different expressions of Paganism. Most of us who identify as Heathens are polytheists who follow some northern European tradition, and in that sense *Heathen* is certainly a more specific word than *Pagan*. But if you prefer to describe yourself as a Pagan, that's an equally appropriate term.

Whether Pagans (or Heathens) call themselves Anglo-Saxon or just Saxon is also a matter of personal taste. There never were any people called "Anglo-Saxons." This is a relatively modern word for the various Germanic tribes who emigrated from continental Europe to what we now know as England. The Angles and the Saxons were only two of these tribes. In the book *Anglo-Saxon England*, Lloyd and Jennifer Laing tell us that when Germanic immigrants stepped onto British soil, they immediately began thinking of themselves as Angles. Meanwhile the Welsh and Romano-British referred to these people as Saxons. So it doesn't really matter if you define your beliefs as *Anglo-Saxon* or just *Saxon*, since both words include the broader indigenous culture of the Germanic people who settled in England. I prefer *Saxon*.

You could, I suppose, even call yourself an Anglish Pagan, although I don't know anybody who does. Those words describe our tradition very well, since Anglo-Saxon spirituality, as it is observed today, is a path that has been preserved in the indigenous literature and folklore of Angle-Land (England).

The term *Anglo-Saxon*, as I'm using it in this book, refers not to race or to ancestry, but to a culture. If English is your primary language, then you are culturally Anglo-Saxon regardless of your personal biological ancestry. If English is your primary language, you *think* in Anglo-Saxon. It probably seems perfectly natural to you that the year is divided into four seasons, right? You might be surprised to learn that the Chinese perceive five such seasonal divisions, and that this perception is equally natural for them. Four annual seasons seem natural to you because English—the language that shapes and defines the way you think—has words for spring and summer, autumn and winter, but no word for the fifth Chinese season that we can only awkwardly translate as something like "Indian summer."

If English is your primary language, much of the *fyrn sidu* is already familiar to you. You've already been introduced to Eostre, the goddess of springtime and the dawn, whose name lives on in a significant vernal Christian holy day. Other Anglo-Saxon deities—Tiw, Woden, Thunor, and Frige—have been hiding in the names you use for the days of the week. The stories you heard as a child spoke to you of the Anglo-Saxon spirits known as elves and dwarves. You already know something, on a gut level, about these entities. The idea of a female spirit who watches over her descendants, called an *ides* in Old English, shouldn't be a strange concept if you've ever heard of Cinderella's fairy godmother. If you remember the story of the shoemaker and the elves, then you already know one mistake to avoid with your own house elves. (Don't give them gifts of clothing.) If you grew up in any English-speaking household, you've been exposed to Anglo-Saxon tradition—to the elder customs—since the day you were born.

People looking for alternative ways of living and worshipping all too often seek out exotic philosophies and overlook what they have in their own backyard. There's nothing at all inferior or intrinsically wrong with Gaelic mysticism, or Chinese medicine or Egyptian religion. But if you don't speak Gaelic, Chinese, or Egyptian, the language and conceptual barriers can be stumbling blocks for those of us who are, for all intents and purposes, culturally Anglo-Saxon.

Take Chinese medicine, for example. Its philosophy and methods have been proven time and again to be effective approaches to healing. But how many of us speak or think in Chinese? How many of us know what it means to have a wind in the head? How do we know if we have a deficiency of liver qi? Most people who use over-the-counter "Chinese" herbs have, at best, only a vague idea what they're doing. There's really no such thing as a Chinese herb. Herbs are just plants. They recognize no cultural, spiritual, or political boundaries. Given the right conditions of temperature, light, and humidity, an herb will grow anywhere on the globe. Ordinary kitchen chives that you can find on almost any spice rack are "Chinese." Marco Polo brought chives back to Europe during his travels. We don't think of chives as Chinese, because they aren't especially exotic. Whether or not remedial herbs are "Chinese" isn't defined so much by the species of the plants as it is by the underlying theories of their use. It's a functional term. An herb is only Chinese when it's being used in Chinese medicine, and the majority of people in the Western world who use exotic herbs today know very little, if anything, about this Asian science.

Chinese medicine is often contrasted with "Western" medicine, even though anatomical medicine (the correct term for the latter) is a relatively recent modality in the Western world. Traditional European healing relied on herbs, diet, and massage, and it was similar in many ways to traditional Chinese medicine. But the European healing tradition is coded into the way we think. We know almost instinctively what it means to "catch a cold," without even considering how absurd that expression must sound to those who don't speak English as their primary language. Every English-speaking person has a fundamental understanding of a pernicious cold condition. It is inherent in our speech.

In the same way, the religion of the ancient Egyptians is truly beautiful and moving, but why not at least consider a spiritual heritage that's already coded into the way you think and speak? The path of the Saxon Pagan is an inspiring but often overlooked journey of honor and strength, wonder and magic. Just as there are similarities between traditional European healing and traditional Chinese medicine, we can find similarities between ancient English religion and ancient Egyptian religion. Both the Egyptians and the Anglo-Saxons perceived what's commonly called the "soul" as having multiple parts. But do you know what the Egyptian *ka* is? Or the *ren*? Okay, then, how about the Anglo-Saxon *mód*? If English is your primary language, you actually do have some gut understanding of this latter concept. You refer to the mód, to the part of your soul that maintains your self identity, in your everyday speech whenever you tell somebody that you're in a good or bad "mood." You already have some understanding of how the Anglo-Saxons defined this facet of the soul, because you speak the language. You know what a mood is, and this gives you insight as to what the mód is.

The people who became known as the Anglo-Saxons actually came from many different Germanic tribes, including Jutes, Franks, Danes, and Frisians, as well as Angles and Saxons. Some of these tribes began immigrating to Britain as early as the third century CE. The first of these served as *numeri* in the Roman army. The numeri were a low-level Roman infantry. Unlike most Roman troops, numeri weren't granted citizenship at the end of their service. They remained legally and culturally Germans. The modern idea of a sudden Anglo-Saxon invasion of Britain is largely an idea promoted by a sixth-century monk named Gildas who deeply regretted the demise of the Roman Empire. Gildas directed much of his animosity at these Germanic settlers who continued to immigrate to Britain in increasing numbers. It's quite possibly true that an army of Germanic fighters revolted after they were denied payment promised by a Celtic warlord, and this event is often perceived as the beginning of an aggressive Anglo-Saxon invasion, but Germanic people had been living throughout much of Britain for centuries at that point in history.

I'm not suggesting that there weren't any disputes or bloodshed in the wake of these Germanic immigrations. Of course there were conflicts. The Roman Empire was crumbling. There was chaos and disorder throughout the Western world. Battles were frequent. But there was also childbirth, the need for food and clothing, and a yearning for song and poetry. When we read *Beowulf* we see only warriors, because that sort of thing makes an interesting story. Nobody wants to read an epic poem about a mother suckling her child, or a farmer tending his fields.

When they could, the Anglo-Saxon immigrants lived more by the plough than by the sword. They farmed the old, fallen estates that remained after the Roman legions left Britain. Bede's description of the Anglo-Saxon calendar in his *De Temporum Ratione* illustrates how important agriculture was for these people. Bede was an eighth-century Benedictine monk whose books preserved much of what we know about the Pagan Anglo-Saxons today. What we don't see in his writing is much that would substantiate Gildas's depiction of the Anglo-Saxons as relentless, uncultured savages. Indeed, hybrid pottery styles prevalent in the late Romano-British period indicate a British attraction to Germanic culture, which would have been highly unlikely in the midst of a relentless, aggressive Saxon invasion.

In the mid-1900s J. R. R. Tolkien presented us with a new set of myths revealing the world of Middle Earth (Old English: *middangeard*) as it was known to the Anglo-Saxons; a world populated with elves and dwarves and dragons, with magic rings and runes and powerful wizards. Although Tolkien's stories are fiction, he drew his inspiration from the world of his Saxon ancestors. Woden himself, chief among the Anglo-Saxon gods, was Tolkien's inspiration for his fictional wizard Gandalf the Grey.

The path of the Saxon Pagan is not a Tolkienesque fantasy, but these stories introduced a vision that's as valid as, and perhaps a little more healthy than, the myth of the "rabid bloodthirsty Saxons." Tolkien himself was a Christian, but he nevertheless preserved his ancestors' values and worldview in his popular narrative. He revealed to us a Middle Earth where all things are bound together by their destiny, and yet the ultimate end is uncertain and determined largely by our personal choices. He revealed a world of magic and wonder and honor. Brian Bates has written an entire book, *The Real Middle Earth*, about the relationship between Tolkien's stories and the world of the Anglo-Saxons. *The Lord of the Rings* may not be a source of knowledge about Anglo-Saxon tradition, but it is a very good source of inspiration.

The world of Middle Earth is so called because it's one of multiple "worlds" known to the Saxon Pagan. The other worlds are extradimensional, but are perceived as being positioned in various directions in relation to our own physical realm. These extradimensional worlds are located above, below, and around our own.

Three of these worlds are the homes or dimensions of the most powerful spirits, including those who we know as gods and goddesses. All three are positioned along the path of the sun, which was perceived as feminine by the Anglo-Saxons, and known to them as the "Glory of Elves."

To the east of Middle Earth, where the sun rises, is the world of Ettinham. The Ettins who dwell there are powerful and sometimes hostile entities. It would be incorrect to characterize them as evil, but they can be dangerous. Despite this, Ettins (also known as giants) are often very beautiful creatures. A variant of the word Ettin is "Ent."

Tolkien's Ents were large, treelike creatures. This is an excellent example of how Tolkien's stories are simultaneously a fantasy and yet also an inspiration for many Saxon Pagans today. Ettins aren't especially related to trees in any way but, like Tolkien's Ents, they are generally aloof and distant from our world. They are primal spirits. If there ever were a War of the Ring here in our real Middle Earth, the Ettins would be unlikely to get involved unless they had some personal reason for doing so. They are alien beings who usually take no interest in us or our world. And on the rare occasion when they do take an interest, their presence is often frightening and destructive. Nevertheless, Tolkien fans should bear in mind that real Ents, or Ettins, aren't "tree shepherds." Nor are they engaged in an endless search for their wives. They are both male and female.

Above us, at the highest point where the noonday sun crosses the heavens, is the world of Osgeard (pronounced "OS-yaird"). This is the realm of the Anglo-Saxon gods. For the Saxon Pagan, the gods are not merely poetic symbols or Jungian archetypes. They are very real entities, as individual and independent as you and I. The Anglo-Saxon gods are easily as powerful as the Ettins but, more importantly, they are defined by their quality of sovereignty. Saxon Pagans recognize that there are many, many powerful entities, but only some of these are acknowledged and revered as our gods and goddesses. We honor them with gifts and devotion, and they, in turn, protect and guide us. In this way the concept of a "god" is almost like a job description. We speak of Woden as a god of inspiration, magic, and battle, because we acknowledge his sovereignty over these facets of our lives. The god Tiw is sovereign over justice and order. Their celestial realm of Osgeard, the gods' land, is so called because most of the gods—the spirits accorded sovereignty—are native to this dimension. Furthermore, the occasional Ettin who fulfills this function of a "god" almost always maintains a hall in the world of Osgeard. Thus we can think of Osgeard as the realm of the gods. The Saxon Pagan often develops personal and surprisingly intimate relationships with one or more of these sovereign spirits. But we'll talk more about them in the next chapter.

In the distant west, beyond the sunset, is the realm of Wanham. The Wanic powers are usually distant, aloof entities. They aren't particularly harmful, but neither are they particularly helpful. Much like the Ettins, they just don't take any interest in our Middle Earth one way or the other, or at least not in the affairs and concerns of the societies that developed in northern Europe. The very few exceptions are the Wanic powers who have their own halls in Osgeard. A story is told in Scandinavian myth of a great war that took place long ago between these families of powerful spirits. It was at the end of this war when the Wanic powers we now think of as gods ascended into Osgeard. But these few are a small minority within a family of great Wanic entities who are, for the most part, unknown to us.

The idea of "other" entities equal in power to the gods may seem odd, but all Indo-European peoples shared this belief. For the Hellenes, these Other Powers were known as the Titans. It's entirely possible that the Saxon gods may be among those spirits who the Hellenes called Titans, and that the Hellenic gods—Zeus, Apollo, Hephaestus, and others—are Wanic powers, or perhaps even Ettins. We simply don't know, nor does the Saxon Pagan have much reason to care. Ours is a specific path, not an eclectic hodgepodge of beliefs. The Wans or the Ettins may indeed be honored as gods by other peoples, but they have no sovereignty in Saxon tradition.

This acknowledgment of Other Powers is a significant distinction between polytheistic religions and paths that deny the existence or divinity of deities other than their own. The definition of atheism as a denial of *all* divinity is relatively modern. Originally this word meant a denial of or disrespect for the gods and goddesses of another culture. Saxon Pagans don't deny the existence of Hellenic gods, or Egyptian gods, or Celtic gods. They are foreign to our tradition, but that doesn't make them any less real or less valid. I've never been to the Louvre and, honestly, don't have much interest in going, but I know that the museum is very real and meaningful to thousands of people. Likewise, I can acknowledge the reality of the Asian goddess Kuan Yin or the Irish Dagda even though neither of these have a place in my religion.

Since these Other Powers are real, sentient beings, it's entirely possible that a Saxon Pagan might have a personal relationship with one or two of them. Many of us find the path of the Fyrn Sidu—of the old ways—after long, convoluted spiritual journeys. If somebody has developed a deep and personal relationship with the Celtic goddess Brighid along the way, it would be more than a little rude to suddenly cut her off. Fortunately our own gods, not being afflicted with excessive jealousy, don't demand this. Of course any imagery or regalia for honoring a foreign deity should be kept separate from the wéofod, or Saxon altar.

Being part of a multifaith household is another reason to honor a foreign god or goddess. If your spouse worships Hellenic deities, then it's appropriate to have both a Hellenic altar and a Saxon wéofod in the home. These, too, would be kept separate, although they might both be in the same room.

Why not just toss all of it onto one altar, with images of Zeus and Kuan Yin and Brighid intermingled with images of Woden and Frige? Why not hold one rite honoring all of them at once? Saxon Pagans avoid anything like this because they believe it is disrespectful. Just because these are all "gods," it doesn't mean that they wish to be acknowledged in the same way. Your grandmother and your girlfriend may both be women, but you don't treat them exactly the same. At least I hope not. Saxon Pagans acknowledge the reality of Other Powers, but we nevertheless remember that they are, indeed, "other."

In addition to the three worlds I have mentioned thus far, there are five other extradimensional worlds or universes that are not aligned along the path of the Glory of Elves. The two most primal of these are found to the north and south of our Middle Earth. These are the elemental realms of fire and ice. The Anglo-Saxons did not acknowledge these realms as true "worlds." They are nevertheless vast and powerful realms. It is said that the cosmos came into being when frost pouring out of the north seethed into fires coming from the southern realm. The resulting alchemical reaction formed the stuff of creation. Since they are not true worlds, the Anglo-Saxons had no names for these realms of fire and ice. But each is populated with its own native spirits. Like the Ettins, the entities who inhabit these realms are sometimes referred to as "giants," but they are nowhere near as intelligent or powerful. And let me emphasize here that they are also in no way sovereign within Anglo-Saxon tradition. They are never worshipped or honored. Not by sane people, at least. In Old English they are called *thyrses*, and although they may have been part of the original act of creation, individually they are purely and entirely destructive. Middle Earth continues to exist only because of the vigilance of the sovereign residents of Osgeard against the destructive powers of frost and fire. The god Thunor, in particular, protects our world from these forces.

The worlds we've discussed so far are, for our purposes, distant from us. The very gates of Osgeard are closed to us and guarded by the god Hama, and the other worlds—those to the north, south, east, and west—are extremely dangerous.

Nearer to our Middle Earth, however, we find the spirit realms of the elves and dwarves. These worlds are located directly above and below our own, and the stories that have survived as fairy tales tell us of mortal men and women who've glimpsed or even traveled into these magical places. The world above ours, Elfham or Elfhame, is a realm of light inhabited by the spirits who nurture the woodlands, meadows, and other natural places. Below us is Dwarfhame, the dark realm of the dwarves. But when we say "dark," we aren't speaking of any negative quality. As we will discuss in a later chapter, the darkness is that of the womb or cauldron where new things are brought into existence. Although these realms are relatively benign, the elves and dwarves aren't necessarily benevolent entities. They can be friendly or hostile, just like other folks we encounter here in our own Middle Earth. But for the Saxon Pagan, approaching them with respect, they can often be useful allies.

Although we have a specific word for dwarf (Old English: *dweorg*), the word *elf* refers to spirits connected both with the world above and the world below. This was traditionally the more common term. Although *dwarf* is a very old word, its usage was rare before the nineteenth century. Dwarves are the "dark elves," which, again, is not intended to suggest that they are innately evil or hostile.

Below the world of the dwarves we find the deepest world where the dead reside. Both the realm of the dead and the goddess who presides over it are known to us as Hel. In what was perhaps the most successful spiritual smear campaign in history, Hel and her domain have been characterized as dark, foreboding, and full of torment. But Scandinavian myths tell us that when the god Bealdor died, the goddess Hel welcomed him into a sumptuous hall within her realm. Hel herself, while sovereign over the dead, is one of the Ettins. It was Woden who gave her rulership over the lower world. What sort of place spirits find upon arriving in Hel's realm is determined largely by what they built for themselves in life. Whether you're going to be received by a multitude of friends or met by an angry mob depends on how you treated those who passed on before you.

Considering the placement of Hel's realm in relationship to the other worlds, the halls of the dead probably are fairly dark much of the time. But then so is Pittsburgh. That doesn't mean either one is a particularly bad place.

Between these extradimensional realms is our own Middle Earth. The physical world. We are, from our perspective at least, at the point of balance between dark and light, fire and frost, creation and destruction. Middle Earth is the physical universe we're familiar with but, like the other realms, it is also a place of spirit and power. Below us are the realms of the dwarves and, deeper still, the halls of our ancestors. Above us are the bright realms of the elves and the gods. Around us are dangerous, alien worlds, but Middle Earth itself is relatively safe and protected.

Middle Earth is the world of the Saxon Pagan. Today Saxon Pagans are found across the globe. Some belong to national organizations, some belong to local tribes or extended families, and some have no group affiliation at all. Some adopt certain affectations of pre-Christian Anglo-Saxon society, while others do not. Some take up traditional crafts such as brewing or weaving, but others have no interest in such things. Even the focus of worship varies; some Saxons devote most of their time to our gods, others are more devoted to their ancestral spirits, and still others focus on the elves, or nature spirits. In polytheistic religions, there is no "one true way" that everyone must follow. On some level, there are probably as many manifestations of Saxon spirituality as there are people who follow this path.

So what's the defining quality of early, pre-Christian English spirituality? What does the "Saxon Pagan" who focuses on magic and the runes have in common with the "Anglo-Saxon Heathen" who directs most of his attention to honoring his ancestors? What's the common denominator between a group of like-minded people dressed in fifth-century tunics, holding a húsel, and the woman in jeans and a sweatshirt who privately offers milk each evening to her house elves?

The one thing that all of these people share is their love and reverence for the Saxon gods.

The Old Gods

In the northern tradition, a god is a powerful spirit who comes from one of three families or tribes. He (or she) may be an Os, a Wan, or an Ettin. Most of the Anglo-Saxon gods are of the former tribe, but there are notable and prominent exceptions such as the Wanic god Ing Fréa and his consort, the Ettin-maid Gearde. What makes a god a god is not his family of origin, but his relationship within Anglo-Saxon culture that grants him sovereignty over some aspect of life or the natural world.

As mentioned in the preceding chapter, a god is a very real, very personal entity. He is not a static, one-dimensional construct. When we say that Thunor is the "god of thunder," we mean that he is sovereign over storms and weather, not that he is limited to this single function. We may not associate him especially with healing or romance or knowledge, but a Saxon Pagan who has a good relationship with Thunor might turn to that deity for help in any of these areas. He's a god, after all. Compared to us mortals, he's pretty darn good at just about everything.

If you were to ask Saxon Pagans which god or goddess to pray to for, say, help in kindling a romantic relationship, their response would be to ask which deities you have the best relationships with. Fréo is a goddess of passion and desire, but if you have never interacted with her, then why should she take any interest in you now? Some people treat the gods—not only our Saxon gods, but the deities of other cultures as well—like divine vending machines, dropping a prayer in the "correct slot" and expecting something to fall into their laps. Not only is this disrespectful, it usually is not very effective. If you have been consistently giving offerings to Fréo and holding rites in her honor, then and only then would it be appropriate to turn to her for help with romance. But if you have been doing this for any length of time, it is less likely that you'd need help with your love life in the first place.

To develop a personal relationship of your own with any of the gods, just sit down and talk with one of them. Begin by offering a gift of some kind. The gods, after all, don't owe you anything. That you live and breathe is evidence that they have already made the first gesture. An offering of mead (honey wine) or fruit juice is usually appropriate as a gift. Depending on the deity, other gifts may be equally appropriate. But mead or apple juice is always acceptable. The former is usually better; however, if you are underage, the gods are not going to penalize you for obeying the law.

I think it is also a good idea to learn something about the gods before you approach them. Otherwise how will you recognize them? Are you going to believe some spirit is Woden just because he says so? (Sadly the answer here is often "yes." A surprising number of people seem to believe that every entity is always unfailingly honest. These same people tend to be the favorite targets of used-car salesmen.) You need to familiarize yourself with the gods if you want to interact with them. Admittedly, the gods are living entities, so what was written about a particular god or goddess twelve centuries ago may not still be true today. Furthermore, they are as multifaceted as ourselves, which means that the same deity can be a stern father, loyal companion, or amorous lover, depending on who you are. Nevertheless, knowing something about a god or goddess will help you recognize that entity, and know what to be suspicious of. If "Woden" says something distinctly un-Wodenish, it may be that he is revealing a part of himself that few people have seen, but it is also very possible that the spirit is not Woden at all.

There is no guaranteed, reliable litmus test for any of this. Very often we just have to accept what is laid before us. This is where common sense comes into play. If your personal experience conflicts with how the ancient Anglo-Saxons related to the gods, acknowledge your experience as a potential truth rather than an absolute truth. We do this all the time in other aspects of our lives. When you hear an unlikely rumor concerning a friend or associate, you acknowledge that it may be potentially true while simultaneously recognizing that it is probably nothing but a rumor. And when we interact with the spirit realm, it's all rumor. The truth behind our interactions, when personal revelations conflict with Anglo-Saxon lore, can only be tested by time and experience.

The typical Saxon deity—if any god can be described as "typical"—is an Os, a spirit from a family of entities whose names are prevalent among place names throughout the English countryside. The god Tiw is commemorated in Tuesley and Tysoe, the god Thunor in the villages of Thursley and Thurston, and the goddess Frige in Fryup. This family of entities, native to the realm of Osgeard, is also revealed in the names we've given to the days of the week. The first two days are named for the sun and the moon, which is appropriate enough considering the important role these two celestial lights have in timekeeping for any pre-industrial people. It should come as no surprise that our English names for these astronomical bodies are the same as the Saxon names for their inherent spirits. Thus the week begins with days named for the goddess Sunne and the god Mona.

Sunne and Mona

Sunne and Mona are often envisioned driving wagons or carts across the sky, much like the Greek solar deity Helios who rides in a chariot. Sunne, the sun, obviously serves as a natural "clock," but for the early Anglo-Saxons, she measured space as well as time. A passage in the Anglo-Saxon Rune Poem describes Sunne's role in navigation when sailors "fare away over the fishes' bath." (The Anglo-Saxon Rune Poem gives a descriptive passage for each of twenty-nine symbols of the Futhorc, a runic alphabet that was used for writing Old English. The Latin alphabet had largely replaced the Futhorc by the time of the Norman conquest. The verses of the Rune Poem describe concepts or mysteries associated with each rune. These inner meanings are the basis for runic divination and magic.) It's very likely that sailors and travelers made offerings to Sunne before embarking on a journey. The sun is at her strongest at the summer solstice, when bonfires were once kindled to honor her.

The god of the moon is called Mona, and while that name looks feminine to our modern eyes, in Old English a final "a" always indicated a masculine name, as in the name of King Penda.

Mona casts a more subtle light, but he was also important to the Anglo-Saxons. This is evident in the abundance of moon lore that has been passed through generations. The early Anglo-Saxons used a synodic (moon-based) calendar in which each month coincided with Mona's cycle of waxing and waning. Even today in the United States—an English-speaking nation and, thus, an heir of the Anglo-Saxons—there are still people in rural areas who know that the dark of the moon is the best time to fish, and who consider the phase of the moon when planting and cultivating their gardens.

Following the two days named for the celestial lights, our week continues as a list of Saxon deities from the family of Oses: Tiw's-day, Woden's-day, Thunor's-day, Frige's-day.

Tiw

Tiw, giving his name to the third day of the week, is the god of justice, oaths, and community. Tiw creates order out of chaos. He is sovereign over the North Star, although he is not, of course, the star itself. Before there were maps and roads and compasses, the North Star was the only reliable nocturnal guide for sailors and travelers. Saxon Pagans often invoke the name of Tiw when exchanging oaths, giving more weight to their words. At one time, thousands of years ago, Tiw ruled the realm of Osgeard, although he has long since passed that duty on to Woden. Tiw is sometimes described as the "Sky Father." This is related to his rulership of the constant stars, and in particular of the North Star. He is also a "war god," because war is sometimes necessary to bring about justice and order.

Tiw's former rulership of Osgeard is a good example of the living, changing nature of our gods. The gods are not static. Their relationships with each other—and with us—can and do change over time. They can even die. This is why your personal experience with a deity may hold true even if it doesn't exactly match what somebody else said about that deity a thousand years ago. The gods change, just as we do. What we experience today will grow into the lore that Pagans will seek out hundreds of years from now.

Tiw has only one hand. The Norse Eddas tell us that he lost the other helping the gods bind a monster called Fenris. The Eddas are Scandinavian stories about the northern Germanic gods. In one of these stories, the dark elves—dwarves—had fashioned a magic ribbon to bind the monster Fenris. But Fenris, suspecting a trick, refused to let himself be tied with the ribbon unless one of the gods placed his hand in the monster's mouth. When Fenris realized he'd been trapped, he bit off Tiw's hand at the wrist.

This story tells us a lot about Tiw's nature. His justice isn't selfish revenge, but rather selfless devotion. To know Tiw is to understand that we sometimes have to make personal sacrifices for our friends, family, and community. Tiw's name shouldn't be invoked when you want to win. It should only be invoked when you want a fair outcome, and are willing to recognize that such an outcome may not work out in your favor.

You will also notice in this story that Tiw was involved in a deception. He was being intentionally, consciously dishonest. There was a price to pay for this, a very steep price, but Tiw was willing to accept the consequences of his deception. This story reveals the heart and soul of Saxon ethics. We are always responsible for our own actions. Everything we do defines us and shapes our destiny.

Woden

The chief of the Saxon gods, Woden, gives his name to the fourth day of the week. He's known by many epithets, including the All-Father, the Old Man, One-Eyed, Grim, and the High One. As befitting the chief god of the Anglo-Saxon pantheon, Woden's name is commemorated more than any other in the names of English villages and natural sites. Wandering the moors and woodlands in his cloak and floppy-brimmed hat, Woden is a complex god whose sovereignty extends from inspiration to warfare to healing to the dead. He is the master magician who discovered the secrets of the runes, and perhaps because of this wizardry his name is often called upon in the old Anglo-Saxon healing charms. As a god of inspiration, Woden equally motivates both the poet and the warrior. It was Woden who gave Hel (herself an Ettin) sovereignty over the realm that bears her name. He rides with a pack of black hounds from the first night of winter at the beginning of November, through the Yule season, gathering up the souls of the dead who have lost their way.

Woden is sometimes characterized as cruel or harsh, but this reputation is largely undeserved. True, if you are looking for a deity who will bolster your ego and make you feel warm and fuzzy inside, this is *not* the fellow to talk to. But that is not because he is malevolent or hostile. It is because Woden has more important things than you on his agenda. He wanders alone, keeping an eye on the balance between the powers that pervade the Seven Worlds, ready to step in wherever necessary to maintain that balance. Woden has two ravens, Thought and Memory, who fly throughout the Seven Worlds each day and bring him news from afar. He acts in accordance with his ultimate plans, which are not always apparent to mortal eyes. But if Woden taps you on the shoulder, it is because he wants your assistance in this great work, and believes you worthy of the task.

If you, on the other hand, do not feel that you are worthy of the task, then refuse it. Don't whine about how "hard" it is to follow Woden, or try to tell people that you don't have any choice in the matter. You always have a choice. Your experience with Woden (or any other deity) may have been a "huge overwhelming moment" for you, but your actions in response to this were of your own choosing. A relationship with any god or goddess is never forced on you.

That I mention this at all should give you an idea of the intense relationships some Saxon Pagans can develop with our gods and goddesses. This is the exception rather than the rule, but it is not uncommon. People who have these deep personal relationships with a deity will often say that they were called or chosen, but of course the final choice was their own.

Thunor

Many people consider Thunor to be the most approachable of the Saxon gods. Known for his fiery temper, especially in his interactions with the fire and frost giants known as thyrses, he is nevertheless a good friend to mankind. With red hair and beard, Thunor gives his name to the fifth day of the week. It is common knowledge that this god (known to the Scandinavians as "Thor") is associated with thunder, but his sovereignty in respect to the fertility of the land is less well known. He is a protector of his people. This facet of his sovereignty includes ensuring necessary provisions as well as martial defense. Although it is Woden who guards the balance of power throughout the Seven Worlds, it is Thunor more than any other god who protects Middle Earth and, more specifically, mankind. Because of this vigilance, his name is often invoked when consecrating or warding any physical space.

Although Thunor is the same god whom the Scandinavians know as Thor, he has little in common with the fictional Marvel Comics character of that name. The latter is an imaginary creation, of course, and I am pretty sure that Stan Lee, the man who created the comic book Thor, never intended it to be an accurate portrayal of a real deity. Stan Lee's Thor is blond, while the real Thunor is notable for his red hair. The comic book character is the son of Gaea (a Greek goddess) and wears a hat with wings that would look more appropriate on the Roman god Mercurius. It is great that the Marvel Comics character has drawn attention to the gods of northern Europe, but do remember that the comic book Thor is only loosely based on the real Thor.

If you have no particular preference otherwise, Thunor is a good first choice for a deity to develop a personal relationship with. Offer him some mead or beer. He tends to be a good-natured god in his relationship with mankind. The hammer, his personal weapon, is often used by Saxon Pagans as a symbol of our spirituality. Hammer amulets were once buried with the dead and hung over cribs for protection. Today they are still often worn as small pendants.

Quartz crystals are also symbols of Thunor. It was once believed that these crystals, known as thunderstones, were delivered into the earth by the bolts of lightning that preceded a loud crack of thunder. A thunderstone can be used as a *wéoh*—a holy symbol—to represent Thunor.

Smaller crystals can be carried or worn as symbols of this strong and protective god.

Frige

The goddess Frige (pronounced "FREE-yeh") is Woden's consort and, thus, the queen of Osgeard. Her name evolved from an Indo-European word meaning "beloved." Like her husband, Frige is a deity of great wisdom. She is sovereign over household and domestic affairs, which were of great importance to the Anglo-Saxons. Don't mistake her domestic interest for subservience. For the pre-Christian English, "household arts" included skills such as the production of clothing, dyes, and medicines. In contemporary society this translates into business acumen. Frige is often a friend to the Saxon entrepreneur. She is a goddess of immense wisdom. The stories about her that have survived tell of Frige advising the other gods, including Woden. Frige's presence can be felt in the boardroom as much as in the home.

Frige is also sovereign over marriages and childbirth. She gives her name to the sixth day of the week. Because of Frige's interest in marriage, Friday (Old English: *Friges-daeg*) was once considered to be a "lucky" day for weddings. In the Christian era, certainly by the 1300s, this changed, and Friday became a bad day to get married, probably because Christ is believed to have been killed on a Friday.

The collective of stars that the Greeks knew as Orion's Belt was known in northern Europe as Frige's Distaff.

Hama and Seaxneat

One Os worthy of mention whose name doesn't appear among the days of the week is Hama. This god protects the realm of Osgeard from intrusion. The Norse knew him by the name Heimdall. It is said that his sight and hearing exceed that of any other god. Some people today acknowledge Hama's sovereignty over liminal places and situations. He is associated with the rainbow, which is the "bridge" between Middle Earth and Osgeard.

Seaxneat (pronounced "SAY-ax-nay-at") is a god whom we know little about, although at one time he was important to the Anglo-Saxons. He apparently fell out of favor for some reason. We have no way of knowing when or why this happened. I mention him here as another example of how the gods are not static ideas. They are living entities who grow, change, and sometimes move on. Perhaps next year Seaxneat will make himself known to Pagan people across the United Kingdom and North America. It is unlikely, but possible. But for now, all we know about him is his name, and that he was an ancestor of the people of Essex.

Evidence suggests that the Wanic powers—the great spirit entities that dwell in the world beyond the western sunset—have been less involved with the English than they have with the Scandinavian peoples. The names of the Wanic gods are absent from our weekdays, and only rarely appear as place names in England. They almost certainly didn't receive as much worship from the Pagan English as the gods described above. If it weren't for a few small but significant clues, there would be no evidence that they were known to the Anglo-Saxons at all.

Fréo

Fréo (pronounced "FRAY-oh") is the undisputed queen of this disappearing act. In indigenous Scandinavian religions such as Ásatrú and Forn Sed, where she is known as Freya, this goddess is deeply adored and respected. It's inconceivable that the Anglo-Saxons would have no knowledge of her at all. And in fact, one small reference about her has survived in Old English literature, specifically in the epic tale of Beowulf. The reference isn't to her directly, but to a necklace known as Brosingamen. Scandinavian lore tells us that this unique necklace was forged for Fréo by four dwarves. There is none other like this necklace. It would be extremely strange for the Anglo-Saxons to be familiar with a piece of jewelry belonging to Fréo and yet know nothing of the goddess herself. This fragment of lore is further substantiated by the personal experiences of many contemporary Saxon Pagans who feel Fréo's presence in their lives today.

Fréo's invisibility may be due in part to the similarity of her name and Frige's. Since it is Frige who's remembered in our word *Friday*, scholars often assume English place names are commemorating her when they very well may take their names from the goddess Fréo. How can anybody be certain which of these goddesses gave her name to a village called Frobury? The problem is further compounded by the fact that the name Fréo (and its Scandinavian form, Freya) is a title rather than a proper name.

It simply means "lady." When the word *fréo* indisputably appears in an English place name, there is no way to know if it referred to this particular goddess, or to some other goddess (who could as easily be called lady), or even to a mortal Saxon woman of high birth.

Thanks to Scandinavian lore, we know that the goddess Fréo is one of the Wanic powers who has a personal hall in the heavenly realm of Osgeard. Fréo is sovereign over abundance and prosperity. It's said that her tears turn to gold when they fall on land, and to amber when they fall into the sea. This fairest of goddesses is also sovereign over physical passion. Along with the god Woden, she has a deep interest in magic, and we are told that she once shared much of her knowledge of magic with him.

Among the Norse, Fréo was most often worshipped by unmarried women, including divorced and widowed women. But men worshipped her as well. Those who would master *wiccecræft* especially, regardless of sex, often prayed and made offerings to this goddess.

In your reading, if you stumble across any reference to Fréo as a "moon goddess," put the book down, or at least recognize it as fiction. Any book that tells of a Norse or Anglo-Saxon moon goddess really belongs in the fantasy literature section of your local library. Neither Fréo nor any other northern European goddess was ever associated with the moon. Why not? Because in northern Europe the moon has always been perceived as masculine! That's why, as a child, you probably heard of "the man in the moon." Not the woman in the moon. If Fréo were to be associated with any celestial orb, the sun, which is feminine, would be a more appropriate choice. In southern, Mediterranean religions, of course, the genders associated with the sun and the moon are reversed.

This is not to say that Fréo is a sun goddess. We do have a sun goddess, as mentioned earlier, but her name is Sunne.

Ing Fréa

Fréo's brother Ing isn't quite as obscure as his sister. He has the distinction of being one of the only two gods specifically named in the Anglo-Saxon Rune Poem:

> *Ing among the eastern Danes was first beheld by men*
> *until that later time when in the east*
> *he made his departure over the waves.*

Ing is depicted in the poem as a traveling god. At the end of winter, an image of this god—possibly a statue—was placed in a wagon and taken around the countryside to ensure a fruitful year. At times, a living woman representing the god's "wife" accompanied the image. The arrival of this image was a time of rejoicing, for Ing, like his sister, is sovereign over abundance and prosperity. Among his many titles are "harvest god" and "wealth giver." Weapons were put away during these processions, for Ing is also a god of peace. It is a sacrilege to bring any weapon into a shrine dedicated to him.

This doesn't mean that Ing is completely opposed to battle. Other titles attributed to him are "battle wise" and "war leader." Battle is sometimes necessary to protect and maintain peace. But then, when the battle is done, it is time to put away weapons and return to a state of peace.

Ing, also known as Ingui Fréa (Lord Ingui), is the ruler of Elfhame, the realm of the light elves who nurture the growth of plants. As mentioned previously, he is described in the Prose Edda as the "harvest god." He took the beautiful Ettin-maid Gearde (pronounced "YAIRD-eh") as his bride, and gave her sovereignty over the cultivated field, which further illustrates his own interest in plants and agriculture.

Ing shares his sister's interest in and sovereignty over physical passion. He is sometimes portrayed as an ithyphallic god. For the Wanic gods, sexual expression is more than just a means of procreation. It is also a sacred celebration of life.

It has been suggested that Ing and Fréo are the "Lord and Lady" of the Wiccan religion. There is no proof of this one way or the other, and yet there are compelling arguments for both sides. The strongest argument against this theory is that the Wiccan Lord and Lady really are not "gods" in the polytheistic sense of the word. Wicca is a *duotheistic* religion. The Lord and Lady are believed, by Wiccans, to encompass all of the divine. In other words, the Lord isn't an individual god but rather an amalgamation of all of the male gods, while the Lady is an amalgamation of all goddesses. This theology is completely different from the traditional Germanic perception of deity, so none of the Saxon gods will fit that particular paradigm. To ask which of our gods is the Wiccan Lord—or which goddess is the Wiccan Lady—is like asking what the color red smells like. There is no correlation. One Wiccan tradition calls upon its Lord and Lady by the names Woden and Freya, but adherents will readily admit that these are just names for a dual godhead that can be called upon by any pair of names—Pan and Artemis, Osiris and Isis, Gwydion and Rhiannon, and so forth.

On the other hand, Gerald Gardner, the man who founded Wicca, was himself an Englishman and thus as likely as Tolkien to be inspired and guided by his Anglo-Saxon ancestors. And there's no question that his initial work in the 1940s was the seminal impetus behind the modern Pagan revival. All Pagan paths today, either directly or indirectly, owe at least some of their inspiration to the Wiccan religion, regardless of how different their theology and practices might be. Was Gardner motivated or directed on a subconscious level by Ing and Fréo? Were they his Lord and Lady? We don't know and, to the best of my knowledge, the principals aren't talking.

Eostre and Hertha

The goddess Eostre (pronounced "EH-oh-streh") is perhaps best known for the Christian holiday that bears her name. That the name of this indigenous English goddess could not be swept aside is evidence of the devotion that the Anglo-Saxons must have felt for her. She is a goddess of springtime and new beginnings, and she was extremely important in the lives of the early Anglo-Saxon immigrants. Agricultural activities—ploughing, planting, shearing—were scheduled around her feast day, which came at the first full moon after the vernal equinox. No weekday bears her name, but in the old Anglo-Saxon calendar, the month of April was known as Eostremonað. This was originally a lunar calendar, since the moon god Mona governed the length of each month, and Eostre's feast day always fell in the month that bore her name. Today, with our fixed calendar, her feast day still usually falls in April, but occasionally comes in late March.

One goddess who must be mentioned here, unusual among the Saxon deities, is the English "earth mother." Like Sunne and Mona, she is unusual in that she is neither Os nor Wan nor Ettin. Nor is she sovereign over the earth; she is the earth itself. This much is made clear in the old Anglo-Saxon charms, in which the earth is invoked as a sentient and potent entity. To the Anglo-Saxons she was known as Hertha or Eorthe.

Within the home, the hearth or fireplace is sacred to Hertha. By association, the kitchen is similarly sacred in contemporary homes where that room is commonly used as a gathering place for the family.

In the Anglo-Saxon calendar, Hreðmonað (March) was undoubtedly named for Mother Hertha. Some scholars have attempted to interpret the name "Hretha" as meaning fame, honor, or she-bull, either overlooking or ignoring the more likely explanation that it is simply an alternate spelling of Hertha. None of those interpretations conflict with the latter theory. Even the she-bull is an appropriate symbol for the earth mother. On the continent, an image of the earth mother was often carried around the countryside in a cart drawn by cattle.

The earth mother is also unique in that she is acknowledged within all Indo-European religions. While her name changes from one culture to the next, her basic qualities remain the same. She is not a sovereign spirit like the other gods and goddesses. Rather than ruling over the earth, she is the spiritual essence of the earth. Unlike the other deities, there aren't a lot of myths describing her exploits. After all, whether we call her Terra or Gaea or Jorðe or Hertha, the earth itself doesn't wander around having fabulous adventures!

Hertha was the first deity I had any personal contact with, and she is largely responsible for me embracing Paganism. My own experience with her was one of those "huge overwhelming moments" that other people often describe. At that point in space and time, she was the One Goddess, permeating all things. I had met some Anglo-Saxon polytheists earlier that year and they had told me about the gods, but I honestly thought they were a bit odd. After my experience with Hertha, however, I felt so content and fulfilled that I lit a candle and gave her my promise that I would follow and honor the old gods.

There was nothing particularly significant about the candle. It just seemed like the thing to do.

———

Now that you know a little about the Anglo-Saxon gods and goddesses, choose one whom you would like to get to know a little better. Thunor is often a good choice, but you may feel an affinity for another deity. Your profession might point you toward a particular god or goddess. Lawyers, judges, and police officers—anyone involved with law and order—may feel an affinity with Tiw. Writers, performers, and people in the military may have more of a connection with Woden. Military personnel could also feel drawn specifically to Thunor, as could farmers and professional athletes. Frige could appeal to almost anyone in business, as well as homemakers and mothers.

Or maybe you share a hobby or personal interest with one of the Saxon gods. If you have a keen interest in gardening, Ing Fréa and Gearde would be deities to get to know. If magic or divination intrigue you, talk to either Woden or Fréo.

Sit down and talk with the deity. This is a form of prayer, but to many people the word *prayer* implies supplication. This is not the time to go begging for something. You are just saying hello. Just visiting, so to speak.

And when I say, "talk with," I mean listen also. This is something we all too often forget to do. Learn how to get your mind into a receptive state. Most of us are not amazing psychics but, by the same token, most of us will occasionally hear or sense something that the gods and elves are trying to say. It may come to you as a voice or a vision, or as an odor that makes you think of something. It may just be an intuition. Or you may get nothing at all, which is okay too. It is not necessary to get an answer. What matters is that, as you speak with the gods, you at least give them a chance to respond.

Don't worry if you do not have a "huge overwhelming experience." That isn't your goal. And looking for that sort of thing will probably lead to disappointment, because most of the time you are not going to get it. People just do not walk around in constant states of divine inspiration. We could not function in that condition.

Also, do not feel that you need to develop a deep personal relationship with the first deity you approach. Or any other deity, for that matter. I have heard people talk about looking for a "patron god," expressing this as if they could not possibly be properly Pagan without some divine sponsor. There are many Saxon Pagans who do not have a "patron." It is far more important that you develop some relationship with all of the gods—at least the primary gods —rather than worry about having a special buddy.

In the next chapter we will look at the *húsel*, a rite used by Saxon Pagans for approaching and honoring a god or other spirit. But content is more important than form here. If you feel moved to speak with a god or goddess, then do so. Don't worry about whether you are doing it the right way. Light a candle if you wish, like I did back in 1971 when I talked to Hertha. Or maybe burn a little incense in honor of the deity you are going to speak to. Any token gesture, given sincerely, will be appreciated. The gods know that you are sort of new to this. Otherwise they would have heard from you before now.

Why not sit down and open your heart to one of the gods right now? Even your wording can be, and probably should be, quite simple. As you make your offering, whatever it may be (and at this point what you offer isn't all that important because, as I have said, the gods and spirits know you are a novice), say something like, "[Name of deity], accept this small gift as a token of my appreciation for all the blessings I have received over the years. I am ready now to follow the elder path, and I welcome your guidance, and the guidance of my ancestors and of the spirits who dwell in this place."

You can speak to our gods anywhere, of course. But many people find that the best place to approach the gods, or the elves or their ancestors—the traditional place—is at an altar. Or what the Saxon Pagan calls his wéofod.

The Wéofod

One nice thing about Old English is that it is very explicit. The language leaves little room for confusion. Recently a friend asked about my opinion concerning Pagan priests, and I had to reply that it would depend on what he meant by the word. In Old English there could be no such thing as a Pagan priest. It would have been a contradiction in terms. The Old English word *préost* is very precise and refers specifically to an ecclesiastic of the Christian religion. In Modern English, of course, it has become much more vague, and different people have different interpretations of the word *priest*.

As a Saxon Pagan, I prefer to think of myself as a *wéofodthegn*. This is another Old English word that means clergy, but it doesn't necessarily refer to a Christian cleric, and there's no question as to the duties or activities it entails. The root of the word is *wéoh*, meaning a sacred image of a deity. The place where the image is kept is the *wéofod*, or altar, and the person who maintains that altar is known as the wéofodthegn.

Obviously you can't be a wéofodthegn without a wéo- fod, but I would go even further and suggest that you can't truly be a Saxon Pagan without one. You can read all the books you like about Anglo-Saxon religion, or Ger- manic myths or about Paganism in general, and I would encourage this. But your religion isn't what you read, it's what you do. The wéofod (pronounced "WAY-oh-fod") is where Saxon Pagans most often conduct or direct their worship. It is their altar. Your own wéofod can be as sim- ple or as elaborate as you wish. But since this is where you are inviting the gods into your life, you will want it to be as attractive as possible.

The first thing to consider is where to set up this altar. The ideal location is a central place in your home where you will pass by the wéofod and its images and tools at least several times every day. In my home, the household wéofod is in the living room. Let's face it, none of us is fo- cused on our spirituality every waking minute. We get caught up in the mundane things that life throws our way. Having your wéofod in a central location where you pass it daily will help you remember to stop and speak with the gods and elves.

I realize that occasionally a person, for one reason or another, simply cannot set up a wéofod—an altar—in a prominent, central location of his or her home. Is it okay to have your wéofod hidden away in a bedroom or closet? Well, that depends on what you mean by "okay." If that is the best you can do, then it is the best you can do. But how would you feel about visiting a friend if you had to sneak in and out a back door? Would you feel welcome? The location of the wéofod should be a place of honor as well as a place where you frequently come. Unless it is absolutely impossible to do so, the gods should be invited into your home openly and proudly.

The "body" of your wéofod will probably be a small table, but any working surface will do. It could be the top of a dresser, or perhaps a bookshelf. The important thing is that you have a clearly defined space to hold your god images and focus your worship. You might want to cover the wéofod with an attractive cloth, either to protect the surface or to give it a nicer appearance, but this is entirely a matter of personal taste.

Obviously the most important thing you'll place on this table or surface is the wéoh, an image representing an Anglo-Saxon god or goddess. But there are a few other things you'll also need. Think of them as tools for connecting with the gods.

Saxon Pagans develop relationships with the gods and elves through a system of reciprocity. Acknowledging the blessings they have received, Saxon Pagans approach the wéofod with a gift for one or more entities. Through reciprocity they then expect to receive future blessings. Note that this is not the same as a bribe. A bribe is something offered on the condition that some need or request be answered. The gift should have no conditions attached to it. It is given freely, in gratitude for blessings already received. But the Saxon Pagan recognizes that the very act of giving creates a bond between the giver and the recipient. It is this bond with the spiritual realms that the Saxon Pagan seeks to build through reciprocity.

Therefore, one thing you will want on your wéofod is an offering bowl. This is where you will usually place the gifts you bring. Afterward, these offerings will be poured or set on the earth, buried, or possibly burned, depending on the gift and the recipient. But the offering bowl is where you will present each gift initially. The bowl need not be expensive, but it should be clean and attractive. If you would not eat out of the bowl yourself without hesitation, then it is not a suitable receptacle for your offerings.

Most people also keep a *récelsfæt* ("RAY-kels-fat") near their god images. This is a small pot or vessel for burning incense. Either loose or stick incense makes a nice, simple offering for daily devotions. The advantage of loose incense is that you can be more creative in your offerings, blending different aromatic herbs. The advantage of stick (or cone) incense is primarily the convenience.

The Saxon Pagan will also usually have a drinking horn on the wéofod. This can be simple and unadorned, or an elaborately carved horn. The simplest version is a hollow cow's horn that has been cleaned out, sterilized, and coated on the inside with beeswax. Liquid offerings—most often mead—are presented in this horn. Hot liquids should never be poured into the horn, as this can dissolve the beeswax coating.

To make your own horn, begin with one that has already been "cored," or hollowed out. These are usually as easy to acquire as uncored horns, so there is no reason you should have to mess with the inside marrow. File

down any rough spots, and then sterilize the horn overnight in a solution of bleach and water. The next day,
wash out the horn with a solution of vinegar and water,
followed by a thorough rinsing with plain water. The in-
terior can now be sealed with a coating of beeswax.

There is no absolute law stating that you have to use a
horn at all. It is what the pre-Christian Saxons used, so it
is favored by many Saxon Pagans today, but you can use
any cup or chalice in the same way. A large ceramic cup
painted with runes can work very nicely for this purpose.
I have a large carved drinking horn trimmed with silver
filigree, but I also use a ceramic chalice when I have liquid
offerings that can't be easily rinsed out of the horn.

Beyond these items and the god image itself, the only
objects that should be on the wéofod are things you will
actively use while connecting with the gods and elves and
ancestors. One or more candles for illumination, perhaps a
set of rune stones if you have any skill with those, or
maybe a rattle or small drum to focus your mind on the
work at hand. Some people find that a rhythmic beat creates an atmosphere conducive to approaching our gods.

The one thing you must have is the wéoh. Otherwise it
is not a wéofod, it is just a table. The wéoh is a symbol of
a god or goddess. It is a focus. Every religion uses foci
such as this. In monotheist religions, the simple act of
folding one's hands together for prayer creates a focus. For
the polytheist, who is not always addressing the same
deity, it helps if the foci clearly indicate *which* gods they
represent. The wéoh is usually a small statue of a god or
goddess, but it can take other forms. Paintings or prints

are suitable. Ideally the wéoh is an actual image of the deity. But if you cannot obtain a statue or painting, and do not have the artistic skill to create one yourself, other objects can be used to represent the Anglo-Saxon gods and goddesses.

Tiw: Any image of a single star, reflecting his sovereignty over the North Star. The rune *tir*, which looks like an arrow pointing upward, can also be used to represent this god.

Woden: A small sculpture of a wolf or raven, two animals that are sacred to him. I have seen the artificial ravens that are sold as Halloween decorations—the better quality ones—used in this way very effectively.

Thunor: The hammer is the most obvious symbol for Thunor. His cart is drawn by a pair of goats, so an image of this animal would also be appropriate. Or use a large thunderstone (quartz crystal).

Frige: Either a simple drop spindle or a weaver's shuttle could be used to represent Frige.

Fréo: This goddess is fond of cats. Just as Thunor has a cart drawn by goats, Fréo's cart is depicted as being drawn by a pair of large cats. So a cat sculpture would be appropriate to represent her. An amber necklace, reminiscent of her magical necklace Brosingamen, is another good symbol.

Ing: On my household wéofod, in addition to my statue of this god, I have a small antler to further represent Ing. To woo his lady Gearde, Ing gave up his sword, and Scandinavian myth arms him afterward with an antler. Any phallic representation is also suitable for Ing.

Eostre: The obvious symbol here is the egg. This needn't be a real egg, since that would quickly rot. Artificial eggs made of polished stone are often readily available in stores that specialize in knickknacks such as this.

Hertha: A small sculpture of a cow can be used to represent the earth mother. Or just a bowl of soil from your back garden!

You should have at least one wéoh, or deity image, but there's no reason why you can't have more. On my household altar I have statues of Woden, Ing, Thunor, and Fréo. Those are the deities I most often interact with, so their images are constantly present. Other symbols are placed on the wéofod when appropriate. For example, in the spring when I make offerings to Eostre, I'll set out an egg to represent her.

If you come from a Wiccan background, you may feel a need to have two images—one of a god and one of a goddess. There isn't any law against this, of course, but in the Saxon tradition there isn't any reason for it, either. As I mentioned in the last chapter, the Lord and Lady of Wicca and the spirit entities revered by the Saxon Pagan are entirely different concepts. Anglo-Saxon spirituality is not focused on a heterocentric paradigm. In the surviving myths we do not, for the most part, see our gods functioning as male/female couples. And a húsel isn't a magic ritual, so there's no need to "balance the male and female energies," a concept that is foreign to Saxon magic anyway. If you must have both sexes represented at your wéofod, I would suggest images of Woden and Frige, or, alternately, the more fraternal relationship of Ing and Fréo. But recognize that this is for your own sense of satisfaction, not because our gods need or necessarily prefer the arrangement.

In my opinion, it is best to begin, at least, with just one wéoh. You can add more later. Choose a god with whom you feel comfortable or with whom you identify in some way, and focus on developing a relationship with him or her. Again, if you don't have any particular preference, Thunor is usually a good choice. This doesn't mean you're limiting yourself to interactions with this one deity. But imagine that you have just moved to a new neighborhood, far from your family and friends. How would you get to know your neighbors? You could throw a block party, but afterward you still wouldn't know any of your guests very well. For that matter, would they come at all? At this point you would be a complete stranger to them. Wouldn't it be more productive to visit one specific neighbor and learn a little about him or her? Likewise, in a romantic setting, which is going to be a more intimate and meaningful experience: a "group date" or an evening alone with that one special person?

This is what you are doing when you put one image on your wéofod and devote your initial attention to that deity. It is a more intimate setting. In time, you should and probably will develop relationships with the other Saxon gods and goddesses. But focusing on one specific deity is a more effective means of building a deep and meaningful relationship than the more promiscuous, shot-gun approach. If you need more than one wéoh for some reason, by all means include a second or even a third. However, you do not get any bonus points for having extra statuary gathering dust, so don't crowd your wéo-fod with a profusion of images.

There is no reason why you can't have more than one wéofod! If you feel a strong affinity for one particular deity, you might want to set up a wéofod, one special altar, just for him (or her) in addition to a second one where you will honor the other Anglo-Saxon gods and goddesses. Or you may want an additional wéofod in your bedroom for eve-ning or early morning devotions. There are any number of reasons for setting up multiple wéofodes. But just as you shouldn't crowd the wéofod with unnecessary clutter, don't fill your home with unnecessary altars. When the sacred becomes commonplace, it ceases to be sacred.

In my home, in addition to the household wéofod, I also have a special ancestral altar. On this, each representative image is a small photograph of a family ancestor. Honoring one's ancestors is important to the Saxon Pagan, as I will dis-cuss in a later chapter. Appropriate items for an ancestral altar would also include pieces of jewelry or other small items that once held special meaning for one or more of your ancestors. On mine I have a wedding ring and my grandfa-ther's fishing knife, along with the photographs. In the cen-ter of the table, surrounded by these symbols, is a single candle and a récelsfæt for burning offerings of incense.

You may want a special altar also for the elves, separate from the wéofod where you connect with the gods and goddesses. A special stone, or a vial of water from a local spring or stream, would be an appropriate focus here. I personally prefer to honor the elves in their own environment, usually in my garden or on the half acre of wooded land that I have reserved for them behind my home, but not everyone has that luxury. Urbanites especially may feel a need to set up altars to honor the elves.

————

It is the act of worship that transforms a table of knick-knacks into a true wéofod. The Saxon Pagan calls this act of worship a *húsel*, meaning a sacrifice, because it always includes a gift.

I have heard it argued that there is no point in giving an offering to the gods, because if they're gods they can surely create for themselves anything you would give them. This argument misses the entire point of the gift. Most of the gifts I have received throughout my life from friends and family were things that I could have obtained for myself. But I appreciated those gifts nevertheless, and the act of giving created bonds of friendship and affection. In the same way, we do not give offerings to the gods because they need something from us. Our gods are not charity cases. We give offerings because the very act of giving creates a bond between the giver and the recipient.

When you are ready to approach a god and hold your húsel, the first thing you will want to do is create a working space around the area of your wéofod, or altar. As we discussed in the previous chapter, not every entity is benevolent. And even the neutral spirits can be a distraction when you are trying to hold a conversation with Tiw or Eostre, or any other deity. So you begin by warding the area to lay claim to the immediate space for the work at hand. To do this, carry a fire around the perimeter while saying,

I carry fire around this holy stead, and ask all spirits to depart unless invited in. Thunor, ward this sacred place.

You do not necessarily need to call on Thunor, but this is the sort of thing he excels at. Furthermore, the fire does not need to be an open flame. You could carry your récelsfæt with its smoldering coal, or even just an incense stick serving as your fire. I most often use a candle or, even better, a small oil lantern. I prefer the actual flame, but sometimes this is impossible, or at least impractical for some reason or another.

After you have warded the area, you will present a gift to whatever entity you intend to honor with your húsel. The choice of the gift will often vary depending on who the recipient is. Mead, beer, or wine are always appropriate offerings. But the offering does not have to be a liquid, nor even something consumable. A small ball of hand-spun yarn would make a wonderful offering for Frige, for example.

The offering also does not need to be tangible. A poem, written and recited by yourself, is a gift that Woden is likely to appreciate. A dance or a song can be offered to Fréo. The value of the gift is not in the form that it takes, but rather in the effort you put into it.

If you have a consumable offering, this should be something you made or purchased specifically to present as a gift. An inexpensive beer, purchased with the intention of offering it to a god or goddess, is better than the dregs from a bottle of Dom Pérignon left over from last night's party. No god or spirit is going to appreciate being treated like your personal garbage disposal.

Address the god or goddess (or other spirit) you are honoring, and explain why you have chosen your particular gift. The words you use are unimportant. As a general idea, you would say something like the following:

> [Name of deity], *I have brought you this* [gift] *because* [why you believe the gift is appropriate].

If you are giving some lager or ale to Thunor, you could say that you have brought it because the old tales have told you that he appreciates good drink. A gift of apple cider to Fréo might include a mention of its amber color, since amber resin is sacred to this goddess. The important thing, however, is that you speak from your heart as you would speak to a friend. Then present your offering.

If you're offering a consumable gift—a drink or some food—it is customary to have a little yourself and then pour or place the remainder in the offering bowl. Drink and food have more meaning when they are shared among friends.

Assuming you are giving a libation of mead or beer or wine, you might say something like this:

> *I raise this horn to you,* [name of deity], *and give thanks for your blessings and guidance. Accept this drink as a token of my gratitude.*

Those exact words would be all right, but they are not as good as something that comes from your heart. But there will be times, frankly, when nothing much is coming from your heart, and at times like that a simple, generic statement similar to the one above is fine. Just remember that if it is a tossup between eloquence or your personal feelings, the personal approach is always better.

Afterward, you may want to conclude your húsel with a few words thanking the deity for his or her time and attention. Pagans who have skill with divination sometimes consult the runes or some other oracle to verify that the deity has, in fact, been pleased by the offering. At the very least, take a few minutes to meditate and clear your mind. Listen for any response the honored spirit might have for you. Most of us have at least some small measure of sensitivity to the spirit realm. But do not worry if you don't feel or hear or see anything unusual. More often than not, you are not going to experience a "great revelation." The important thing is that you open your mind to the possibility.

I can't emphasize this enough: Being Pagan is not about what happens to you. It is not about what you believe or what you read or what you think. It is not about having spectacular revelations. Being Pagan, purely and simply, is what you *do*. The gods are not going to drop everything and focus on you to ensure that you have some kind of epiphany. If they have something to say, they will say it, but most of the time that is not going to happen. Nor, in the greater scheme of the universe, does it matter. Getting a vision or intuitive impression does not mean you are a better Pagan than the next guy. In fact, it may very well mean the exact opposite. When I had my experience with Hertha back in 1971, it was not because of any virtue or accomplishment on my part. She was not there to praise me. She came to help me. I was a pathetic mess at the time. When you hold a húsel, remember the expression "no news is good news."

So you have presented your offering, spoken with the deities or spirits, and given them an opportunity to respond. Now you will need to complete the rite by disposing of the offering in some way that the deity or deities can easily receive it. This is the beauty of an intangible offering such as a song or a poem—it is gone as soon as it has been presented. Tangible offerings need a little more work. Drink is usually poured out onto the earth. Food can be either buried or set outdoors somewhere, but be sure you don't leave any food offerings where they will attract unwanted vermin. Other, nonconsumable tangible offerings should either be buried or burned. Do not dispose of these nonconsumable offerings in the garbage. They are not trash. Solid food offerings should only be disposed of in the garbage if there is no other alternative, which may be the case for some urban dwellers.

A crafted offering such as a small knife or piece of jewelry might be broken as it is given away. Alternately, such an item might be cast into a swift stream or a deep pool of water. Whether broken, buried, or burned, the important thing is that the offering is removed from human use. It is literally given up to the spirits.

That is all there is to it. You may eventually decide to add other flourishes—specific prayers, a favorite song, a guided meditation—but everything else is icing on the cake. The essential part of a húsel is the act of giving, with the knowledge that every gift demands a reciprocal gesture.

How frequently Saxon Pagans hold húsles depends on how much time they can commit to their gods and ancestors. Many of us make some small daily offering, but a full húsel each and every day usually is not practical. Weekly is not too often. There are other religions, certainly, that honor their gods every week without fail. A lot of Saxon Pagans choose to hold monthly húsles. And if you cannot devote some time at least once a month to honoring your gods, are you really Pagan at all? Or is it more of a hobby, something to read about or talk about?

The idea of giving selflessly is diametrically opposed to the "gimme" attitude seen in some alternative spiritual paths today. You may be asking yourself, "What's in this for me?" Maybe you need a better job. Or you might be single and hoping that your situation will change at some time in the future. What about your own needs?

Consider this: if you have developed a good relationship with a few of the gods, don't you think they are going to be looking out for you? We go out of our way for those we care about. On the other hand, we are less inclined to go out of our way for people who only talk to us when they want something. Why should we expect the gods to be any different?

In my experience, the people who follow "gimme" philosophies—the people who pray to a love goddess when they need love, then forget her and turn to a prosperity god when they need money—are not terribly successful as a general rule. You may have met somebody like this, a person who is perpetually casting spells and "working with" this or that god to get something he wants, and yet he always seems to be unemployed or incapable of making a relationship work. You may even be this person. If the "gimme" approach hasn't worked for you in the past, perhaps you owe it to yourself to try something different.

I am not saying that you should never, ever ask for a boon. Piety doesn't make anyone immune to bad fortune. There will undoubtedly be times when you really need some help or advice, and at those times you should turn to the gods with whom you have developed some bond. But be sure to develop that bond first.

This illustrates another quality of the offerings given in a húsel. These are gifts freely given, out of love and respect, not as payments or bribes. Saxon Pagans give to their gods not for what they may get in return, but in thanks for what they have already been given. It is our gods who gave the first gifts—the stars and the mountains and oceans, the rising and setting of the sun and moon. It is our ancestors who gave us our blood and bones, our language and our names. It is the elves who nurture the plants that feed and clothe us.

Saxon Pagans don't approach the spirits with a beggar's bowl in hand. They come proudly forward, bearing gifts and shaping their own wyrd through honorable acts.

Honor and Wyrd

Saxon Pagans' most valuable asset is their own honor. This is what shapes their *wyrd*, or destiny. They take full responsibility for their words and actions, recognizing that these are what define them as human beings.

Honor is not the same thing as morality. A moral is a rule or law governing behavior. It is finite, limited, and inflexible. "Don't tell lies" is a moral. The inflexibility of morality tends to create a need for endless qualifiers. We all know that there are times when it is better to lie than to speak the truth. For example, Aunt Maggie really does not want to hear that her new dress is hideous, no matter what you may actually think. So you tell her how nice it looks. Or, if you cannot go that far, you at least refrain from telling Aunt Maggie that the dress looks like something a demented clown would wear. Because the truth is not always appreciated or even desirable. Admittedly, the world might have been a better place if we had all been more honest about leisure suits back in the seventies.

"Don't kill others" is one moral that multitudes of people abandon when any nation goes to war. It might be argued that we could eliminate a lot of horror and grief if people actually adhered to this moral, but the fact is that there are countless exceptions to the admonition against killing. Almost every nation throughout history, including our own, has routinely killed criminals. And few people would consider it an immoral act to kill in defense of a child or loved one. For that matter, most of us cheered when we watched Luke Skywalker blow up the Imperial Death Star, without any thought for the many innocent workers and technicians he killed. That was a fictional event, but in our gut we recognized and acknowledged it as a "good" action. Morals are situational.

Honor, on the other hand, is a way of living. It is a state of being. Saxon Pagans are usually true to their word, not because of an arbitrary moral, but because this behavior—honesty—strengthens their word and their honor. And this, in turn, shapes their wyrd in a positive way.

Wyrd is the Old English word that evolved into our modern word "weird." Its meaning has changed significantly through this transition. It is often defined as fate or destiny, but these concepts are only approximate. To understand wyrd, we must look to its source. Wyrd is a process that continuously occurs in the present moment, unfolding and flowing from a person's *orlay*.

Think of orlay as everything—every action, thought, and word—in your past. I have heard some people poetically describe orlay as all of the things that we have placed in the Well of Wyrd (which will be discussed shortly). It is all of those things we have done that have shaped who we are. You could think of your own orlay as the source or seed of your "personal wyrd."

A newborn infant initially inherits its orlay from its parents and ancestors. This initial orlay is its heritage, compiled from the words and deeds of those ancestors. It is what the infant starts out with. And while that might not seem completely fair, it is no secret that we are all dealt different cards when we come into this world. A child can also acquire orlay through adoption. The adopted child receives orlay from both adopted and biological parents, but the initial orlay comes through the two people who contributed to the genetic composition of the child's body. The entirety of the child's orlay, whether from a biological or adoptive parent, is reflected in the environmental, psychological, and physiological factors that inevitably shape the child's development.

From this point on, we build upon our initial orlay, adding additional layers through our words and deeds. The words and deeds of a young child tend to have little consequence, and they have equally little effect on the orlay. But as the child matures, his or her own actions become more and more important. Thus we each have the ability to sculpt our orlay, adding layer upon layer, much like the way an oyster can transform a rough grain of sand into a beautiful pearl. This is accomplished by living with honor, and choosing the right actions and words to the best of our ability.

Going back to the example of honesty, Saxon Pagans try to speak the truth because they know that their words, once uttered, become part of their orlay forever. There are no "take backs." If you constantly lie, your words will lose their power and meaning until eventually you don't have any faith in them yourself. This is why we say dishonest people have "broken" their word. (Remember how all of this is coded into our language?) Things that are broken have less use or value. If you break your word often enough, it becomes entirely worthless.

Does this mean the Saxon never tells a lie? Of course not. He would not be so rude as to crush Aunt Maggie's feelings. But he is more likely to avoid saying something that would hurt her than to openly lie, and if he does need to say something blatantly untrue, the Saxon Pagan does not pretend that nothing has been broken or compromised in the process. There is always a price for breaking our word. It does not matter what justification we may feel that we have for lying. We still lose a bit of our integrity. The result may be well worth the cost, but the cost is still there, nevertheless.

This same principle extends to our actions. Your best intentions do not excuse your deeds. Everything you do becomes a part of your orlay. It becomes a part of who you are. People who are industrious, hospitable, and generous of spirit are rarely unhappy. I am speaking in general terms, of course. There are times when each of us will experience extreme sorrow or misery. But those who have laid strong, positive deeds into the Well of Wyrd are more likely to attract strong, positive experiences into their lives.

The Well of Wyrd can be thought of as the source of all creation. As your words and deeds shape your orlay, they become a part of this eternal pool. The Eormensyl, the great tree that connects the Seven Worlds, rises out of the Well of Wyrd. The waters of this well nurture the roots of the Eormensyl and sustain it. And so whatever you lay down in the well not only shapes your orlay, but also ripples outward to touch everything throughout the cosmos. You may hear people speak of a "web" of wyrd when they describe this concept of interconnectedness.

As adults, most of our orlay is built through our own efforts. But just as orlay can be acquired through adoption, we can also take on the orlay of others in different ways. A very common way is through marriage. When we say "for better or worse," we had better mean it, because each spouse acquires the orlay of the other. Even when a marriage fails and ends in divorce, the two parties are changed, forever, by the union they once shared.

Likewise, any oath that binds us to another also binds us to that person's orlay. Whether you are performing a ritual of blood brotherhood, being initiated into some secret society, or joining a Pagan group, you should carefully consider the wording of any oath before taking it. Does it bind you to a specific person? If it binds you to a group of people in general, what reputation does this group have? In other words, do you really want to weave your orlay with that of the other person or group? The answer may very well be yes, but give it some thought before taking an oath you might regret later.

You should protect and nurture your orlay at all times, because it is the source of wyrd. Wyrd is not a thing, but rather a process. As I mentioned, it is sometimes envisioned as a web connecting all things. Everything has some minute effect on everything else (a phenomenon that is sometimes called the "butterfly effect"). Your wyrd does not unfold independently. It is influenced by the wyrd of everything around you. A collective force rises from the Well of Wyrd, flowing through the branches of the Eormensyl. Thus unexpected things can happen to us, and when they do, we are very likely to describe them as … weird.

What you can and do affect directly, every single day, is your own orlay. Through honorable actions and words, you can shape this in a way that strengthens the part of your soul that the Saxon Pagan calls the *mægen* (pronounced similar to "Mayan"). This, in turn, affects your wyrd, causing it to unfold in a stronger, more positive way. The mægen is your spiritual power. The amount of mægen you have is directly related to your orlay. Whenever you act in a way that harms your friends or community in any way, no matter how you try to justify it, you lose some of your mægen. When you speak falsely, you lose some. Conversely, honorable acts and truthful words build mægen.

To consciously apply this to your life, you have to be painfully honest with yourself. An honorable act is one that strengthens or benefits your friends, family, or community. It is not something that benefits you personally. If you do a favor for somebody because you want their love or friendship, that is not an honorable act. It is not particularly dishonorable, but that person's love or friendship is the payback. You gave, you received, end of story. But going out of your way to help somebody and expecting nothing in return would be an honorable act. Volunteer work for a community charity is an honorable act. Fulfilling a promise even when it is inconvenient to do so is honorable act. The payback is mægen.

Do you see a connection here between honor and the Saxon húsel? When we give to our gods without expecting anything specific in return, we are acting honorably. We are building mægen, or spiritual power. But honor is not something that begins and ends at the wéofod. Your orlay is the culmination of all your actions and words. It is everything you say and do, every hour, every day of your life. It is not enough to hold an occasional ritual, or say a prayer. You have to walk the walk.

The reverse—actions that harm your family, friends, or community—are dishonorable. And again, this does not only apply to people or groups you want to impress. The measure of your honor is what you offer to others when there's no immediate return. The lore of our ancestors tells of our gods walking among men to see for themselves how a stranger is received. On a metaphysical level, your mægen is weakened with every dishonorable act. Whenever you treat a stranger rudely, you lose some mægen. When you steal something, whether it is from another individual or from a corporation, you lose mægen.

Your orlay, the sum total of your actions and words, constantly regulates how much mægen you have.

If you observe people around you, you will often see this principle in action. Those who are always "looking out for number one," even if they seem outwardly successful in some ways, are rarely very happy.

When determining whether or not behavior is honorable, Saxon Pagans often look to certain ideals or *thews* as general rules to guide their actions. These are not the same as morals. They're descriptions of virtues that Saxon Pagans strive to incorporate into their lives. There are variations of these thews, but they are usually nine in number. I should point out here that there's nothing in the Old English poems and stories about nine thews. They were undoubtedly inspired by Ásatrú's Nine Noble Virtues (another modern convention), but they are nevertheless good guidelines to keep in mind.

1. *Respect*. For others as well as for yourself. These two forms of respect tend to go hand in hand. Those who truly respect themselves are more likely to extend that respect to others. Saxon Pagans know it is dishonorable to be disrespectful of others, even if they disagree with other people's opinions and choices.

2. *Piety*. Consistently giving offerings and reverence to the gods and spirits. Piety is the defining quality of a Pagan. When the indigenous European religions were initially persecuted, beginning with the Religio Romana, the first laws enacted against them forbade the offering of sacrifices to the gods. These

laws struck out at one of the most fundamental traits of Pagan religion. When people could no longer make offerings, the cycle of reciprocity with their gods and ancestors was broken. Piety is an active expression of honorable behavior toward our gods, our ancestors, and the elves.

3. *Courage*. Here we mean courage not only in facing danger, but in facing daily challenges. Courage is not the same as a lack of fear. In fact, without fear there can be no courage, because courage is the act of responding honorably to fear. The fear need not be a fear of physical harm or danger. We should also strive to react courageously and honorably when confronting a fear of failure, or a fear of rejection.

4. *Generosity*. Giving to others freely. This is a core value for the Saxon Pagan. When you give of yourself, whether the gift is money or effort or your time, those acts become part of your orlay. This was so important in Anglo-Saxon society that a person's rank or importance was once directly related to that individual's personal generosity.

5. *Good demeanor*. This not only means being polite, but also facing adversity calmly and rationally. This is very similar to the thew of courage, but without the element of fear. Good demeanor is the act of responding honorably to an annoying or frustrating situation. It is very often related to the thew of respect when the source of annoyance is another person.

6. *Hospitality*. Both toward one's guests and, conversely, one's host. When somebody enters the home or domain of a Saxon Pagan, a contract is established between host and guest. The host is obliged to make the guest feel comfortable and at home. The guest, in return, is expected to be respectful toward everyone in the household. Again we see a connection with the thew of respect. Long ago, before there were Holiday Inns and Sheratons, travelers depended on the hospitality of others for a dry place to sleep. Today we are not expected to open our homes to strangers, but when we do open our homes, we are honor-bound to extend hospitality to our guests. Some Saxon Pagans, as a symbol of this hospitality, make a point of offering drink or food to any guests who enter their homes.

7. *Loyalty*. Remaining true to friends and family under all circumstances. Bear in mind, however, that "remaining true" does not mean you have to condone or defend dishonorable behavior. Remember that we are talking about honor here, not unyielding rules or mores. Sometimes loyalty has to be mixed with tough love. Nobody has to suffer abuse from another, or put up with lies or other dishonorable behavior. This is not the same thing as loyalty. Loyalty is how you behave, not how the other person behaves. There will always be some people who try to make us feel responsible for their behavior. Saxon Pagans should never betray their folk, but neither do they have to defend a friend or kinsman

from the consequences of that person's own actions, unless oathbound to do so. Nevertheless, Saxon Pagans are ever loyal to their folk.

8. *Mindfulness*. Being conscious of all your actions and their possible consequences. This ties in with what we have already said about orlay. Saxons know that they are always responsible for their own actions. These actions become a part of who they are, in a very real way, shaping their destiny forever. Saying "I didn't know" or "I didn't mean to" does not change a thing. It is your responsibility to know. To be mindful means to consider all possible outcomes of what you are about to do.

9. *Truthfulness*. Being true to your word. Your words, like your actions, become part of your orlay. You have heard the expression "He's as good as his word." Honorable people can be trusted by those who are worthy. When they lie, honorable people are painfully aware that they are breaking their word. They will avoid doing so whenever possible.

Each of these thews—these nine ideals—helps to build and strengthen your mægen. By aiming toward these ideals, you can and will improve your personal orlay and the wyrd that unfolds from it. In fact, once you understand the process of wyrd, you will not even have to think about these thews, because you will be able to identify honorable actions in almost any given situation among your friends and family, and within your community.

When I say community, I do not just mean your physical community. The thew of piety specifically reminds us that we need to honor and acknowledge the spirits, including our gods. When we think of spirits, our thoughts usually turn to those who dwell in the worlds beyond Middle Earth, but our own world is also populated with spirit entities—the elves—toward whom we should exercise thews of respect, hospitality, and mindfulness.

The Elves

The word *ælf*, which we now pronounce as "elf," refers to a discarnate or disembodied spirit, in contrast to a wight (Old English: *wiht*), which can be any entity—a nature spirit, a god, a human, an animal, an ancestor. An elf is a purely spiritual being. In its most general sense, as an umbrella term for "spirit," this can include entities such as dwarves and *púcan*, which will be described later on.

In a more specific sense, the word *elves* refers to the nature spirits, or "land wights," who dwell in the world around us. These are the beautiful entities who were the inspiration for the fictional elves in Tolkien's stories. They have a connection with the world of Elfhame, and many travel freely between that realm and our own Middle Earth. Some are quite powerful and might be viewed almost as demigods. Others are delicate and timid. Although they are creatures of spirit, they are quite real, and Saxon Pagans approach them with the same respect as they would any other being.

The Anglo-Saxons recognized the relationship between elves and the natural world, and they classified these beings according to the ecosystems they nurtured. There were woodland elves (*wudu-elfen*), mountain elves (*dun-elfen*), sea elves (*sae-elfen*), plains elves (*feld-elfen*), and so on. These words describe functions or relationships, and they are very similar to the Swedish classifications of nature spirits. The words don't represent different species. Although an elf may have a deep affection for an ecosystem, it isn't physically bound to any one location. A woodland elf can abandon its forest home and become a mountain elf, or vice versa.

The god Ing was given rulership over the elves long ago. He is the lord of Elfhame. As Ing's folk, the elves nurture the growing things in their respective ecosystems. And like their lord, they abhor needless bloodshed. Elves often vacate an area where blood has been spilled needlessly. A place abandoned by elves will have a lifeless atmosphere pervading it.

These spirits are not the diminutive, winged fairies that were imagined by Victorian artists. They are powerful beings, often larger than men. In the oldest descriptions, they are often said to be a tall folk, like the Irish *sidhe*, who I suspect are simply another tribe of what we Saxons call elves.

Sometimes the elves are called the Good Neighbors, since they share our world. In the pre-industrial era, when the productivity of the land was crucial to survival, people went out of their way to establish positive relationships with these unseen neighbors. The Saxon Pagan still does this today. Although few of us now have an agrarian lifestyle, we are nevertheless a part of Middle Earth, and the natural spirit forces around us are no less real than they were a thousand years ago.

To learn more about the elves in your locale, go outside and learn something about the land around you. The dominant physical features of the landscape are a good indication of what the local elves are like. You are not going to find many mountain elves on the plains of Kansas! Invest some time in exploring your environment, not just once, but repeatedly and at different times of the year. Notice the birds, insects, and wildflowers. If you live in a wooded area, learn to recognize the different trees. Notice the difference between a hickory and an oak or a walnut tree, until these become familiar at a glance. If you live near the seashore, watch the tides until their patterns become as familiar as the back of your hand. Become aware of the world around you.

This isn't an idle, tree-hugging exercise. In our human world, you would scoff at anyone who claimed to be good friends with a neighbor whom he had never actually seen face to face. It is equally difficult, if not impossible, to develop true relationships with the elves if you have never bothered to do more than glance at their physical reflections. If you would know the elves on any intimate level, you must know something about their world. You must become familiar with Middle Earth.

When you approach the elves, do so with the utmost courtesy. Despite the expression "Good Neighbors," the attitudes and behaviors of elves are as varied as our own.

At one time it was commonly believed that many illnesses were caused by hostile elves, and the old Anglo-Saxon healing charms include some intended to cure ailments such as "elf-shot" or "the water-elf disease." This does not mean that elves are evil, of course, but they do have different temperaments and personalities just as we do. Elves should be approached with the same caution you would have with any stranger.

One way to approach the elves is with a húsel, exactly as you would honor the gods. Offer them a gift. You could do this at your wéofod; however, I think it is better to seek out these spirits in the locations they naturally frequent. You could invite wood elves into your living room, but for your first contact, at least, wouldn't it be more polite to go out to the woods? Where exactly you go and what sort of elves you contact depends on the physical features of your local area. If you live near the coast, you could give an offering to the sea elves. If you live inland, look for a special grove of trees, or a stream or natural pond, or perhaps an unusual rock outcropping.

As for the choice of an offering, there is no easy answer. Elves have their own personalities, just as we do, so what will please one may leave another unimpressed. Corn meal, bread, fruits, and semiprecious stones are all usually received favorably.

Omit the warding. If you have gone into their natural environment, this is not your home, it is theirs. It is rude to walk into somebody else's house and tell everyone to get out. Here, at whatever place you have chosen, you have come as a guest of these land wights.

As you would do in a húsel at your wéofod—at your altar—speak from your heart. During your first contact, introduce yourself to the elves and express your intention to establish a cordial relationship with them. Ask them to let you know if there is anything they want or need. Speak your words aloud. There is a power to the spoken word. By voicing your thoughts, you give them form and substance. You might say something like:

> *Good Neighbors—you spirits of the land and air and water—I am* [name], *and I come to you in friendship. I ask for nothing but your sufferance in return, for I desire to learn of you and your ways.*

Again, this is only a suggestion of what you might say. The words should be your own. You are conversing with the spirits, not reciting a magical formula.

After you have spoken to the elves, present them with your offering. How you do this will depend on what you brought with you and where you are. Offerings to sea elves or river elves can usually be dropped directly into the water, assuming the offerings aren't toxic. Offerings to wood elves, mountain elves, or plains elves are typically left on the ground. But if you brought a food offering, be sure that you aren't breaking any local ordinances. Municipalities often have laws about leaving food out, because it attracts and encourages vermin. If this is an issue, consider an offering of cut flowers instead.

For most of us, the dwarves are less apparent, but they are no less real. Like other elves, they can be found within this middle realm although they have a connection with a world other than our own. The world of the dwarves, their own domain, is below our Middle Earth.

Dwarves are spirits who bring "potential"—whether we call it spirit or inspiration or ideas—into manifestation. This is why we have traditionally envisioned them as smiths. Dwarves make things. It was four dwarves who made Fréo's necklace Brosingamen. It was dwarves who brewed the original mead of inspiration. Dwarves crafted Woden's spear and Thunor's mighty hammer. This is their function. They bring things into manifestation.

From their realm below, the dwarves manifest gold and silver and gems. The realm below, within the dark soil, is also where a seed's potential is transformed into a living plant. Other elves, light elves, may nurture the growing things around us, but it is the dwarves who initially bring them into existence.

Their world, Dwarfhame, is the dark womb of creation. Its residents have personalities as varied as those of the elves. And, much like the elves, they aren't always benevolent. Just like elves, these spirits are capable of causing disease and misfortune. They are also equally capable of becoming valuable friends and allies. Craftsmen and artisans are especially likely to seek out the friendship of dwarves. But since these spirits are often found in the world around us, anyone can benefit from developing a positive relationship with them. Dwarves are also valuable allies for entrepreneurs. It was very common for Indo-European cultures to associate the world below with riches. If prosperity is one of your goals, it doesn't hurt to befriend a few dwarves.

Popular folklore imagines a dwarf to be short and stocky in build, but this is at best a generalization. Some people report experiences with dwarves who are quite large. There may be some correspondence between stature and power, but in any event the dwarves (and all other elves, for that matter) have no real physical form in this world, so their "size" is a subjective perception on our part.

A húsel for the dwarves is very similar to one for any other kind of elf. You don't need to concern yourself as much with location as you would for wood elves or sea elves, because dwarves have a different sort of function. They are not as connected with the physical features of the landscape. Nevertheless, if you have seen or sensed a dwarf in a specific locale (as people often do) then it makes sense to hold a húsel at or near that place.

Another difference is timing. Dwarves don't care for sunlight, so a húsel for these spirits should be conducted at some time after sunset. This is not strictly necessary, but it should be intuitively obvious that these dark elves prefer to be approached in darkness.

The most appropriate gift for a dwarf is one you have made yourself. The function of dwarves is to bring things into manifestation, so you honor them when you emulate this. A wood carving, sculpture, or piece of jewelry would make an excellent offering if you have the skill. A loaf of bread you baked yourself is equally appropriate. Your gift could even be the performance of a story or song, if the story or song is one you created yourself. The important thing is that the gift be your creation. It should be something you have personally brought into manifestation.

As for the final disposal of your gift, I think this should be self-evident, but let me mention here that burial, in my opinion, is the very best way to complete the offering of tangible gifts to dwarves. There is no hard rule about this, however. I have been to a húsel where offerings to the dwarves were cast into a bonfire.

So far we have looked at spirits found primarily outside our immediate homes. One type of spirit that a Saxon Pagan always tries to develop a good relationship with is the house elf. These elves were also known to the Anglo-Saxons as *cofgodas*, or "chamber gods," and in later folk tales they are often called brownies. These diminutive spirits have an affinity for human dwellings, much as other elves associate themselves with natural outdoor features. But they are real spirits, like other elves, and can come and go as they will. Folklore tells us a great deal about the house elves, probably because they interact so closely with us. We know that they are almost always small in stature, at least from our own subjective viewpoint. They often have little patience for lazy or sloppy people. They can be productive and helpful when they are happy, but troublesome when they are annoyed. And they are very likely to leave a residence if offered inappropriate gifts.

Overall, we're given the impression that they are highly temperamental. But I think that this is mostly because of proximity. It is much easier to get along with somebody if you do not actually live with that person, and this seems to apply equally to the spirit world.

If you do not feel like you have a good relationship with your house elves, begin by cleaning up the place a little. You do not necessarily have to be a neat freak, but at least make your bed and pick up after yourself. To paraphrase an old expression, house elves help those who help themselves. Time and again we see examples in folklore of household spirits who leave or harass the slovenly mortals they live with. So put your dirty clothes in the hamper, clean out the cat's litter box, wash last night's dishes, and see if that makes a difference.

Beyond this, you can build a connection with your house elves as you would with any other spirit. Since house elves live in our homes, rites to them are usually very simple and informal. Small daily offerings are not uncommon. But for house elves, the nature of the gift is very important. You may have heard the story of the shoemaker whose house elves disappeared after he and his wife offered them a gift of clothing. These spirits should only be offered food or drink. Milk is almost always appreciated as an offering, although I have known people to offer them beer, mead, or even whiskey. Slices of bread or cake make good food offerings.

Offerings to the house elves are one exception to the "don't throw it out" rule. Burning these offerings is obviously impractical, and burial would result in countless little food graves around the outside of your home. The small offerings you give to your house elves should be left out overnight, and then disposed of as you would dispose of any other leftover food.

If you are worried that these gifts of food might attract vermin, offer them in glass-covered containers. A glass covered cake dish is an attractive way of presenting the offering.

There are words describing other kinds of spirits, but it must be remembered that these terms or classifications always describe a function. The term *púca* ("POOH-ka") describes a mischievous, troublesome spirit. It is not a specific race. Your own house elves can become púcan if they're annoyed with you. A púca in the home may manifest as poltergeist activity. Or the spirit may steal small objects, which usually reappear later in unexpected places. Because of this latter habit, some people today refer to these púcan as "borrowers." Outside the home, púcan sometimes mislead travelers.

A *mare* ("MAR-eh") is an elf that harasses people in their sleep. This is where we get our word *nightmare*, which, contrary to common belief, is a word completely unrelated to horses. Folklore tells us that maran sit on the bodies of sleeping people, crushing them and causing them to have bad dreams. The traditional charm for driving away the mare is a stone with a natural hole in it. The stone can be worn in a pouch or hung over the bed. Nailing a horseshoe on or over the bed is also said to offer protection from maran. The protective power of horseshoes, and iron in general, is a very old belief.

The habit of classifying elves by function continued well into the medieval period. In northern England, the term *boggart* was used for any spirit that frightened people. Whether or not that was the spirit's intention didn't even factor into this. There was no distinction made between the benign spirit who just happened to startle somebody, and the true boggart who haunted a well or side alley. Púcan were considered boggarts if the trouble they caused was in any way frightening.

I mention spirits such as púcan and maran to illustrate again that elves are not necessarily the friendly, benign creatures that some people seem to think they always must be. Friendship is something earned; it is not something that other folk—whether they are mortal beings or spirit beings—owe you. Elves are very much like living people; most of them are quite decent, only a few are openly hostile, but almost all of them expect a degree of respect.

As a term for any discarnate entity, the word "elf" also includes human spirits. The Saxon Pagan makes offerings to these spirits, too, or at least to some of them. In the next chapter, we will look at ancestral spirits and their place in our lives.

Those Who Have
Gone Before

When we speak of ancestors, most people automatically think of their blood ancestors. But an ancestor can be any predecessor or forerunner. Here we are using the word to mean any person whose existence or actions were responsible for bringing you to where you are today. At one time these people would almost always have been blood ancestors, but this is not necessarily true in our contemporary, mobile society. Hence there are different kinds of ancestors, many of whom are not genetically related to you (at least not in any measurable way). In the greater scheme of things, since we all affect each other indirectly to some extent or another, "ancestors" can be said to include the entirety of the human race.

As with the elves and dwarves, the spirits of the dead aren't necessarily friendly. The Anglo-Saxons approached the dead with caution. The Old English word *orc*, often translated as "demon," meant a spirit of the dead. The word comes from Orcus, one of the names of the Romano-British god of the underworld, and may have been introduced into Old English by soldiers serving as Roman numeri. Orcs were considered dangerous by the Anglo-Saxons, and with good reason. Imagine you are a Saxon man or woman living in the fifth century. A ghost may have found itself in that condition when your father swung his scramasax into another warrior's chest during a battle. Such a ghost would obviously harbor some resentment for your entire family. Tolkien, of course, used the word *orc* to describe a fictional race of brutal, warlike, and generally nasty humanoid creatures. His use of the word reflects the early Saxon apprehension of the dead. In an era when battles and raids were commonplace, the Anglo-Saxons were well aware that the dead, as often as not, could be hostile and potentially dangerous.

Some people might argue that we live in an entirely different world now. But if you were to encounter a spirit today, who would it be? Consider the random assortment of entities the average, contemporary American citizen could stumble across. One such entity might be the spirit of a Native American whose nation was obliterated by European settlers. Or the spirit of a German soldier killed by American troops in World War II. Or perhaps a British soldier who died while trying to prevent an uprising in what we now know as the Revolutionary War. But war is not the only source of dissension among men. Other entities could be hostile due to conflicts of race, religion, or even sexual orientation. If the presence of a ghost doesn't make you at least a little nervous, you are not being entirely realistic.

This in itself is sufficient reason to connect with one's ancestors and try to establish positive relationships with them. It is good to have allies in the spirit world.

While there are many kinds of ancestors, it is only natural for us to be more immediately aware of our blood ancestors. After all, these are the people who gave us the color of our skin and hair and eyes. They bequeathed to us all of our physical virtues and weaknesses. Unless you were adopted, you inherited a surname from an ancestral bloodline, as well as your language and culture and many of your personal habits.

Reverence and respect for one's blood ancestors has always been important in Indo-European cultures, including those throughout northern Europe. Saxon Pagans believe that some human spirits continue to watch over their descendents, often for many generations. These ancestral spirits can be valuable guides. It does not matter whether you knew these ancestors in life. You may very well have a long-dead great-great-great-great-grandmother who still keeps an eye on you. Saxon Pagans try to nurture their relationships with their blood ancestors, just as they do with their relationships with other spirits. The difference is that we each have an innate connection with our blood ancestors that we do not automatically have with the gods and the elves. You are your ancestors' legacy to the future, so they have reason to take an interest in your well-being.

Nevertheless, some people find it difficult to honor their blood ancestors. We haven't all been blessed with strong, positive family relationships. But "ancestor," as you have seen, does not have to be an immediate relative. In fact, dictionary definitions suggest that the relationship should be at least more distant than that of a grandparent. Furthermore, we are not honoring our ancestors because they were perfect, but because they brought us to where we are today. And that, to some extent, includes an acceptance and forgiveness of their flaws.

When looking at your blood ancestors, it is absolutely essential to focus on the proverbial drinking glass as half full rather than half empty. No matter how awful your childhood may have been, you would not exist at all if it were not for your blood ancestors. They gave you your bones and sinews. Unless you were placed for adoption at birth, they gave you your language. It was your blood ancestors who gave you your orlay. More importantly, what your ancestors may or may not have given you before has nothing to do with how they could help you *now*.

Even when people have good relationships with their families, some may feel awkward honoring blood ancestors who were not Pagan, thinking that this may be offensive to those ancestors in some way. I do not see why this should matter. You are just showing them respect. If you had a child of your own who converted to Christianity or Judaism or Islam, would you want to be forgotten? Your own spiritual orientation is unimportant here. This is between you and your ancestors, not between you and the gods.

It also doesn't matter whether or not your personal blood ancestors were English. When honoring blood ancestors, you are showing respect to individual people, not to a culture. If you are a Saxon Pagan of Italian or African or Japanese descent, you may wish to honor the Anglo-Saxon people as your *spiritual* ancestors, but you should also honor your own blood ancestors. They have brought you to where you are today, and at least some of them are still likely to be watching over you.

But what if you were adopted? Your blood ancestors have nevertheless contributed to where you are today, of course. You have a genetic inheritance and, on a meta-physical level, your blood ancestors bequeathed to you the orlay you came into this world with. Were it not for your blood ancestors, you would not exist at all. Let me hasten to add that the importance of your adoptive parents cannot be overemphasized either. Through the process of adoption, a child also acquires a degree of orlay from his or her adoptive parents. This, in turn, connects the child to the adoptive parents' blood kin and ancestral lineage. Ancestors of the adoptive lineage can and should be honored just as you would honor blood ancestors, because they are equally as responsible, if not more so, for bringing you to where you are today.

In addition to ancestors of blood or adoption, we have ancestors of spirit. These ancestors, sometimes called ancestors of the heart, are those predecessors who are unrelated to us in any way, but who are nevertheless responsible, in part, for bringing us to where we are today. Their actions have somehow shaped our lives, either directly or indirectly.

Some ancestors of spirit were among our personal mentors in life. They may have been our teachers or former employers, or maybe just older people who befriended us when we were children. They inspired or influenced us in some way. This inspiration may have come through the advice they gave us, or by the example of how they lived, or a combination of both.

For the most part, the idea of ancestors of spirit is a modern phenomenon. Fifteen hundred years ago, any personal mentor would almost always have been a blood relative. People just didn't move around as much back then. It was very common for a man to spend his entire life within a ten-mile radius of where he was born. Everyone in his village was related to him in some way. An ancestor of spirit was almost always simultaneously a blood ancestor. Today we live in a much more mobile society, and the personal mentors who shape our lives are very likely to be people who we aren't related to at all by blood.

One of my own spiritual ancestors is a former employer who passed away from this Middle Earth in the mid-1980s. She was a remarkable woman, stronger in spirit than anyone else I've ever known. Today I still often turn to her for advice. In life, she had a great influence on me, second only to my parents and grandparents. This particular ancestor of spirit taught me to have more self-confidence, and to reject the limitations that other people and institutions would impose upon me. I would not be the same person now had she not shaped my ideas and goals.

Ancestors of spirit may also be more distant historical figures. The most obvious examples are the Anglo-Saxon tribes of pre-Christian England. All Saxon Pagans—even if we haven't a drop of English blood in our pedigree—honor these people to some extent, because we quite obviously would not be where we are, spiritually, if it were not for them. Their gods and traditions are the heritage we embrace today.

But there may be other historical figures among your personal ancestors of spirit. These need not always be as ancient as the Anglo-Saxons. A woman, for example, might consider early feminists like Susan B. Anthony or Amelia Bloomer to be her spiritual ancestors. A gay man could accord the same honor to Richard Leitsch, Leo Martello, or Ed Buczynski. Anyone who shaped your life in any way, directly or indirectly, is an ancestor of spirit. It is entirely appropriate for Americans to honor ancestors of spirit such as Thomas Jefferson or Benjamin Franklin.

Yet another type of ancestral or forerunner spirit is the human spirit associated in some direct way with the land you live on. Superficially these spirits vaguely resemble elves in function, but they are a class unto themselves. Ancestors of the land are the spirits of the men and women who lived for most or all of their lives in your immediate area. Like ancestors of spirit, the idea of ancestors of the land is a very modern concept, a by-product of our highly mobile society. Wherever you live, generations of other people lived there before you. They developed the land, pouring their sweat and love into it. They literally became a part of the land as their skin cells sloughed off and fell into the soil. Their hair and nail clippings likewise went into the land. Before we took up the practice of encasing our dead in solid vaults, these people's entire bodies returned to the land they had once lived on.

If your family has lived in the same region for generations, then your ancestors of the land are your own blood ancestors. Otherwise they are an entirely separate class of ancestors that you should also remember to honor.

Reverence for ancestors is so important to the Saxon Pagan that it becomes the central focus for his or her worship at certain times of the year. Perhaps the most sacred time for revering one's ancestors is Mothers' Night, the night of the winter solstice. Mothers' Night marks the beginning of the Yule season, a time of celebration that continues throughout the next twelve days. The night of the solstice is the longest night of the year. On this night, Saxon Pagans honor their *idesa*, the female ancestors who continue to watch over them.

I usually offer my ancestral mothers either mead or wine, and I like to honor them by reciting my matrilineal heritage as far back as I can. I begin with Sally Harris Rice, a pioneer woman who settled in the Missouri wilderness in the early nineteenth century, and then I work my way through the generations, mother to daughter, ending with my maternal grandmother. Naming these individual ancestors makes the rite more meaningful, more real, for me. But it certainly is not necessary. If you do not have names and details of individual female ancestors, you can address them collectively as "mothers of our mothers."

You may hear somebody describe Mothers' Night as a time when the Great Goddess gives birth to the Sun God. Where do I even begin? The problem with this misinterpretation is not just the idea of a masculine Sun God, which is entirely foreign to how northern Europeans perceived our solar orb, but also the concept of the sun being "born" at the winter solstice. The vision of pre-Christian people cowering in terror because they are afraid of the dying sun is utterly ridiculous. By the time anyone is old enough to formulate any view of the order of the universe, that person is going to be thoroughly familiar with the seasons. Nothing in the lore of northern Europe suggests a belief that the sun is reborn annually. And who is this Great Goddess allegedly birthing the new sun on Mothers' Night? For the polytheist, the gods and goddesses are persons. They have names. The Anglo-Saxons, like the people of other ancient cultures, never worshipped anything like a generic, nameless Great Goddess. In Bede's writings (our source of information concerning the origins of this holiday), both the Anglo-Saxon name—*Módraniht*—and his own Latin description clearly indicate that Mothers' Night is a celebration of multiple mothers, and distinctly a celebration of ancestral spirits, rather than any single entity.

Mothers' Night was once a time to specifically honor blood ancestors but, as you have seen, modern Pagans also have ancestors of the heart or of the land who they are not genetically related to. After I have honored my matrilineal heritage, I like to include a few words of thanks to the ancestor of spirit who I mentioned previously, and also to my Aunt Alma, who I am related to only by adoption.

Here is a simple rite—a húsel—that you can hold on Mothers' Night:

Gather everything you will need, including whatever you want to offer to your female ancestors. As always, mead is an appropriate offering, but a nice wine will work equally well. Cider is also a good seasonal choice, especially when spiced as a wassail drink, as described later in this book. You may want to decorate your wéofod with pinecones, holly boughs, or mistletoe, but this is a personal preference. Or, for a change, you could hold your húsel in front of your Yule tree, assuming you have set up an evergreen tree in your home in preparation for the holidays. For those of us who follow the old Saxon ways, the tree is symbolic of the great tree, the Eormensyl, that connects the Seven Worlds. Since you are reaching out to spirits who dwell beyond the borders of Middle Earth, and since you conveniently have a large tree standing in your living room, this is as good a place as any to make your offering.

Ward the area by taking a candle or small lantern around the room while saying, "Thunor, I ask you, ward and protect this holy place." In belief systems influenced by ceremonial magic, the sacred space is always a circle, but the shape is irrelevant here. If you are in a small, square room, you have a small, square space to ward. It also does not matter what direction you follow while carrying the flame. Again, this is a religious rite, not a magical working. Go whichever direction—clockwise or counterclockwise—that is most convenient for you.

If you want to burn some incense, this is the time to do it. Light the coal or the stick or cone, and place it in your récelsfæt. Now take a moment to think about your idesa, your female ancestors. As I have said, these do not have to be women you knew in life, although those women may certainly be included in your meditation. Nor are the honored idesa necessarily limited to your blood ancestors.

If you have brought drink as your offering, lift the horn or chalice up as if presenting it to a loved one, which is exactly what you are doing. (Adapt this as necessary if you have brought an offering in any other form.) Take a small sip of the drink and say something like,

Mothers of my mothers, I stand here before you with love in my heart. You in whose wombs my folk were quickened, you who have watched over my kin, nurturing and giving and protecting; on this night I do honor you. Accept this gift as a token of my gratitude, and know that you are remembered by me and my household.

Pour the remaining drink into the offering bowl, saying, "*Éala tha módra.*" If the Old English is in any way awkward for you, just substitute a modern "Hail the mothers." Personally, I feel a cultural connection by using some Old English in my rites, but you should never let language become a barrier to communication.

The following day, any time after sunrise, take the offering bowl outside where you can pour out the libation directly onto the earth.

———

Another time of year when many of us focus on our ancestors is Halloween. We do not know if there is any historic precedent for this. What we do know is that the Saxons celebrated this time of year as the beginning of winter. It marked the beginning of the "blood month," when all of the excess livestock would be slaughtered. Regardless of historical veracity, because this is such a liminal time, it seems appropriate to remember and honor our ancestors, whether they are ancestors of blood, of adoption, of the heart, or of the land. Many Pagans feel a connection with the realms beyond Middle Earth at this time of year. The world itself is beginning to die around us. It is a time of transformation.

Our ancestors can be honored at any season, of course. For some Saxon Pagans, reverence for the ancestors actually takes precedence over worship of the gods or honoring the elves. But we give offerings and praise to all of these spirits—gods, elves, and ancestors—for the same reason, to ensure that we are "right" with the universe.

If all of this is confusing at first, it is perfectly fine to honor all of the spirits with a single offering in your daily devotions. In fact, every one of us does this at least once in a while. We get busy with life. It is better that you pause each day to remember the spirits with a simple, brief offering, rather than just give up because there is too much to do.

For a simple daily devotional, offer a natural herbal incense. Use an incense like lavender or rosemary, rather than some artificial concoction sold as "Hot Jungle Love" or "Rainy Day." This incense is something you can keep handy on your wéofod. Stick or cone incense is especially convenient, but some people prefer to use loose aromatic herbs and sprinkle them over a burning coal.

Light the incense and say,

I give this sweet herb to the elves who live in this place, to the ancestors who have brought me to this place, and to the gods who have blessed this place. Accept my gift, and know that you are remembered by me and my household.

Remember, though, that this is a bare minimum. Periodically you should make time for the gods, or for the elves or your ancestors, and hold a true húsel. Make time to really speak to the spirit or spirits who you are honoring, and to listen for what they may have to say in response.

The Magic of
Middle Earth

No matter how many offerings you have made to the gods and your ancestors, sometimes things go wrong. Or sometimes, when things still have the potential to go right, you just do not want to leave it up to pure chance. At times like these, the Saxon Pagan will very likely turn to what people today commonly refer to as magic.

Traditionally this would often involve a consultation with the local druid. Many people automatically think of the Celts when druids are mentioned, but the Anglo-Saxons also had their own druidic tradition. Saxon druids (Old English: *drý-mann*) probably filled the role of teachers, at least for some of the other tribesmen. Like their Celtic counterparts, the Saxon druids were keepers of lore for their villages, preserving knowledge in a predominantly illiterate society through extensive memorization. There were undoubtedly cultural differences between the Celtic druids and the drýmenn. But the fact that the Anglo-Saxons borrowed the Celtic term suggests that there were also significant parallels.

The Saxon druids were, above all else, wizards. In fact, because almost every surviving Old English reference to the drýmenn depicts them performing some work of magic, the word *drýmann* is often translated as "sorcerer" or "magician." The Anglo-Saxons had around two dozen words that could be translated as "magic." *Drýcræft* (druid-skill) very likely included quite a few of these other *cræftes*, much as our modern science of biology includes other "ologies," such as zoology and physiology. A druid's skills may have included *scinncræft* (ghost-skill, or mediumship), *lybcræft* (drug-skill, or medicine), and *tungolcræft* (star-skill, or astrology), among others. He may have worked *galdorcræft* (spells) or practiced *wiglung* (soothsaying). Each of these skills is one facet of the larger, more general concept that today we refer to as magic.

The importance of a concept in any culture is reflected by the number of words relating to it. The plethora of Old English words for magic reveals how commonplace these skills were in the lives of the Anglo-Saxons. If magic had not been such an important concept for the Anglo-Saxons, they wouldn't have evolved so many ways to describe it.

The lack of a single umbrella term for magic gives us further insight into the Anglo-Saxon perspective. The skills that we would describe as magic were not considered occult or extraordinary. Magic was so commonplace that it did not warrant a special name. It was an integral part of Anglo-Saxon culture. Lybcræft, skill with drugs, for example, makes no distinction between pharmaceutical effects and magical effects. Herbs and other medicinals were once routinely administered with complex magical chants to help ensure their efficacy. And tungolcræft, the skill or knowledge of stars, is an Old English word that can be interpreted equally well as either astrology or astronomy.

Most Saxon Pagans today have at least some familiarity with magic, but this word—*magic*—describes a variety of skills. As with any other skills, experience and study are invaluable; however, some measure of innate talent is also involved. Not all of us are destined to become world-renowned chefs or best-selling novelists. And not all of us are destined to become masters of the druidic arts. In fact, within any Saxon Pagan community, the percentage of real drýmenn, or druids, is going to be fairly small.

Are you one of those few? I don't think this is something we should try to define about ourselves. It is not as if being a drýmann makes you a "better" Pagan. You do not need to know a thing about magic to follow the path of a Saxon Pagan. Nor does knowing a little about runes or herbs or *galdor* make you a great drýmann. This is a distinction that others should bestow upon us, not something that we assume for ourselves. Don't give yourself a title that you may later need to defend. If others in your community think of you as a drýmann and come to you consistently for magical aid, that's fine. But it is also fine if your contributions to your community manifest through other, less mystical means.

For most of us, "magic" becomes a part of our lives in small but nevertheless important ways. These can sometimes be difficult to identify, because much like our spiritual forebears, we do not always distinguish between the magical and the mundane. Most of us have had a personal interaction with at least one god or goddess, or with our local elves, but many Saxon Pagans would deny that there is anything magical about this. Some people might even consider the húsel itself to be a magical act in a very general sense. Although we do not have any specific end result in mind when we make an offering to our gods, we do assume that there will be some form of reciprocity. Those of us who travel through the real Middle Earth often do not even notice these minor manifestations of magic around us. We are constantly immersed in what many people would consider a world of wonder and enchantment, but for us it is just a way of life.

Throughout this chapter, I am using the word *magic* to describe any practice that creates an observable effect without a physical cause. This is admittedly a concept that would be entirely foreign to a fifth-century Saxon, who would make no such distinction concerning cause and effect. I only mention it here to differentiate these skills from "magic" exercises and practices that are intended to induce subjective personal transformation.

Galdor

The use of words, spoken or sung, is a potent magical skill for those who possess both training and talent. Tolkien depicted this frequently in his stories. His fictional elves worked healing magic through song, while the Black Speech of Mordor had a similar power to wreak havoc wherever the dark words were uttered. Here again we see how Tolkien drew his inspiration from the customs and beliefs of his

Anglo-Saxon forebears. And as English-speaking people, we still understand the power of vocalization today. It is in our language. When we speak of individuals working magic, we say they have "cast a spell," using a noun that evolved from the Old English verb *spellian*, meaning "to speak or proclaim."

The art of working magic through vocalization—casting spells—is called galdorcræft, or "sound-skill." The use of galdor (sounds) is often combined with other cræftes. As suggested earlier, the Saxon herbalist is very likely to use a spoken charm while brewing a potion. Likewise, the druid may sing over runes while consulting their wisdom. Galdor can be a powerful tool for shaping the magic of Middle Earth.

Even now, people try to tap into the power of vocalization with things like "positive affirmations," which utilize the spoken word to create changes in one's life. Saxon Pagans likewise consider everything they say, knowing that their words are as important as their deeds. Can you see why it is so important that you not break your word? And beyond this, it is also important that we not inadvertently give power to negative influences through our words. If there is something about yourself that you do not like, avoid labeling yourself in that way. Words are an act of creation, giving form to intangible ideas.

Galdorcræft takes this to an even higher level, using time-proven techniques to imbue words with additional creative power. One such technique is alliteration, the repetitive use of a sound at the beginning of each word, as in "Peter Piper picked a peck of pickled peppers." Alliteration is, in fact, a defining quality of Old English poetry, more important than rhyme. Repetitive sound gives more emphasis to the words used in a charm.

Suppose you live in or near a coastal city and have heard reports of a hurricane coming in your direction. Naturally you hope that the damage, if any, will be minimal. Consider the following two statements:

Let the hurricane do little damage to [name of city].

Versus...

By wand and word I work my will to ward this warren. Wind be still!

Which of these has more force behind it? The repetitive use of sound in the second statement creates an almost hypnotic effect. The first statement is a positive affirmation defining your desire, but it does not have much drive behind it. It fizzles.

If you are familiar with the Anglo-Saxon runes, you may have noticed something else about the second statement. The repetitions are the sound represented by the *wynn* rune, a rune of prosperity and contentment that also has defensive powers. And so the statement is further empowered in an entirely different way. This is more advanced, but it is a good example of how different cræftes, or skills, can be woven together.

We often encounter alliteration as seen in the preceding example in Anglo-Saxon magic charms. A tenth-century charm intended to ease a sudden stabbing pain included a line saying, "The smith sat and crafted a little knife." In the original Old English, however, this was, "*Sæt smith sloh seax lytel*." Again we have that hypnotic, repetitive quality, this time sounding almost like the hissing of snakes.

Another galdor technique frequently seen in the Anglo-Saxon charms is the narrative style. A story grabs and concentrates our attention much more than a simple description. A person who has absolutely no interest in the Civil War will sit and watch and listen enraptured for two or three hours if those same events are presented in the form of a blockbuster movie. The narrative style takes advantage of our natural inclination to focus on a story. The Second Merseburg Charm, as translated by Bill Griffiths (1996, 172), is an old but well-known healing charm that tells the following tale:

> *Phol and Woden travelled to the forest.*
> *Then was for Baldur's foal its foot wrenched.*
> *Then encharmed it Sindgund (and) Sunna her sister,*
> *then encharmed it Frija (and) Volla her sister,*
> *then encharmed it Woden, as he the best could:*
> *As the bone-wrench, so for the blood-wrench, (and) so*
>   *the limb-wrench*
> *bone to bone, blood to blood,*
> *limb to limb, so be glued.*

The narrative has nothing to do with the person who needs help, but it focuses attention on the possibility of healing with a spoken charm. We also see some Other Powers—greater spirits other than those revered as gods and goddesses—in this charm, specifically the sisters of Sunne and Frige. The narrative tells of these entities healing the wrenched foot of a young horse. Finally, at the end, the most important words are spoken—bone to bone, blood to blood—to promote healing in the current situation.

If the disease is believed to have spiritual origins, typically caused by an elf or dwarf, the charm may be a narrative of the healer meeting with that spirit's relatives and making a pact or agreement in which the spirit desists. In another charm I've translated from the *Lacnunga*, a tenth-century compilation of Anglo-Saxon medical remedies, this one to heal a dwarf-induced disease, the narrative tells us:

> *Then came the creature's sister,*
> *Then she concluded it, and swore oaths*
> *That never again would this hurt the sick person.*

The narrative style can be a very effective galdor technique. Buckland's *Practical Candleburning Rituals*, first published in 1970, uses the narrative style in some of the spells presented within its pages. As you can see in the examples here, narratives need not and often do not directly address the situation. In this way it differs dramatically from positive affirmations. A narrative describing a third party can be especially powerful, because it disinvolves the ego. If illness has left you nauseous, for example, the last thing you want is to hear somebody telling you how great you feel. The Saxon narrative style distances you from the issue, making it easier for the galdor to take effect.

Faring Forth

The ability to journey beyond our Middle Earth is known as the art of faring forth. This is another field of endeavor that one may or may not consider to be magical, depending on how you define the latter. At the very least, faring forth is a form of divination. Often this is as far as it goes. The practitioner travels beyond Middle Earth to gain some knowledge or insight.

The Saxon Pagan recognizes that what we call the spirit or soul is actually a collective of different things. The part sent out while faring forth is called the *fetch*. Usually this takes the form of an animal, although I have heard that the fetch can occasionally appear as a person of the opposite sex. The fetch journeys beyond Middle Earth to realms at once alien and mutable. Very often the practitioner has no memory of the journey after the fetch returns. During the session, the practitioner will often answer the questions of others who are present. In this way, faring forth can be thought of as divination or soothsaying.

Where exactly the fetch travels varies depending on who you talk to. The really good practitioners usually refuse to attempt to define it. This isn't a façade of mystery. Faring forth is an extremely subjective experience. If you are the sort of person who analyzes everything to death, it is unlikely that you will ever excel at this. The talent for accepting experiences for what they are, without trying to imbue them with some order or meaning, is crucial to the practice. Those who are really good at walking between the worlds understand this. So practitioners may share their subjective experience, saying something like, "It felt as if I were descending," but a good one will not pretend to know, objectively, where the fetch has journeyed. This is one measure of a practitioner's integrity. If somebody tells you that his fetch has traveled to the Well of Wyrd, or over the rainbow bridge to speak with the gods in Osgeard, be cautious of the visions he shares with you. The well he sees may indeed be the Well of Wyrd, but it could also be symbolic or representative of something else. This is especially important when a practitioner is faring forth on behalf of someone else. Some practitioners do not have the ability to convey their experiences without applying their own meaning and interpretations. A querent who brings a problem before the practitioner may find mountains of meaning in the vision, but for the practitioner himself, the vision of a cigar should always be described as nothing more or less than a cigar.

Faring forth may or may not be a group activity. In a group there is typically a practitioner, at least one querent, and often, especially when there are multiple querents, an assistant whose job is primarily to maintain order. It is important that the assistant be a person whom the practitioner trusts implicitly. While faring forth, the practitioner is extremely vulnerable.

The practitioner usually takes a seat in a comfortable chair. It is important to sit upright. While faring forth, the practitioner is in a semiconscious state, and the sitting position lessens the possibility of him drifting completely into sleep. He is then covered with some kind of cloth, at least over the head and shoulders, to separate him from the mundane world. The covering is often a cloak that the practitioner wears when he first takes his seat. This covering reduces distractions. I have heard practitioners say that the very act of covering the head can itself become a ritual inducing a trancelike state. In the darkness, under the cloth, the practitioner is free to release his fetch and send it forth.

Once he is ready to begin, the practitioner begins to concentrate on his breathing. A common pattern is to inhale through the nose to a count of four, hold the breath to a count of four, and then exhale through the mouth to a count of four. By concentrating on his breath, the practitioner attunes himself to his *æthem*, which binds together his body and the various parts of what we refer to today as his "soul." Intentional, focused breathing helps the practitioner loosen his æthem and send out his fetch. Occultists often refer to the æthem as an "astral cord."

The assistant needs to be familiar enough with both the practitioner and the process to know when the practitioner is ready to answer questions. At this point, he allows one person to come forward at a time. The querent sits or kneels in front of the practitioner and presents his question. There is no guarantee as to what will happen next. Hopefully the practitioner will give the querent an answer. And hopefully the answer will actually make sense to the querent in some way.

If an answer is forthcoming, it is rarely direct and to the point. Faring forth, after all, is not the spiritual equivalent of a Dear Abby column. The practitioner, if he is truly skilled, is not likely to say, "Your suspicions about your husband are unfounded. Trust what he's telling you." The response will be more like, "I see a ring…a gold ring…bathed in sunlight." This is what separates the mediocre practitioners from the really good ones. The latter response is a pure vision that may have some meaning to the querent that the practitioner himself does not understand. In the former response, the practitioner has taken his vision and applied his own interpretation to it.

The assistant also needs to be familiar enough with the practitioner to know when enough is enough. Traveling between the worlds can be exhausting. As a rule of thumb, three questions should be the maximum for a beginner. But even a skilled, experienced practitioner has his limits, and the assistant must be ready to step in and bring the session to a close. At this point the assistant will often help the practitioner summon his fetch. Again, this is accomplished primarily through focused breathing. When the fetch has returned and the practitioner's head is uncovered, he can be offered a cup of mead or some small cake or bread to eat. This is not just a symbolic gesture; it helps bring the practitioner fully back to Middle Earth, grounded and whole.

The art of faring forth can be practiced alone, but it is more difficult. The disadvantage is that there is nobody to witness the experience, so the practitioner must be conscious of his own visions. Because of this, he is not as free to completely let go of his fetch. Otherwise the process is very similar to that described above. The practitioner finds a comfortable seat, covers his head with a cloth of some kind, and focuses on controlled breathing to loosen his æthem and release his fetch. It is still important to avoid assigning any meaning to visions that come during the session itself. These visions can be analyzed later, but at the time it is critical that the practitioner simply accept and remember them.

As described above, faring forth is a method of divination, or a means of extending one's perception. Many people would consider this "magic," but it is subjective and thus exempt from the definition we are using. But faring forth can be also used in a more active sense by a skilled practitioner if the fetch is sent forth to affect some objective change here in Middle Earth.

Wortcunning

A wort (Old English: *wyrt*) is any plant, and so wortcunning is the knowledge and lore of plants. It is similar to herbalism, although the latter term does not necessarily include any knowledge of the spiritual nature of plants. The ancient Anglo-Saxons understood that spirit is found in everything. In the old Anglo-Saxon herb charms, the plants are addressed as sentient, spiritual beings. This spiritual aspect is not just acknowledged in wortcunning; it is fundamental to the practice.

Wortcunning is similar to lybcræft (healing skill) in that it does not distinguish between magic and medicine. Lybcræft, in fact, required an extensive knowledge of plants, as these were the predominant source for healing materials. If an herbal poultice relieved chest pain, it did not matter to the Anglo-Saxon healer if the effect was pharmaceutical or magical. The end result was all that mattered. Similarly, whereas today the herbalist is limited to teas, poultices, and salves, a master of wortcunning will often use plants in ways where there is no physical correlation between cause and effect. The distinction between wortcunning and lybcræft is that the former uses herbs for both healing and nonhealing purposes, and the latter uses "substances," herbal or otherwise, to affect changes in the body. Obviously the two often overlap.

Let me state very plainly here that neither lybcræft nor wortcunning should ever be considered substitutes for modern anatomical medicine. This is not just a legal disclaimer; it is something I sincerely believe. I do not pretend that anatomical medicine is perfect in every way, but it has proved to be a wonderful advance for mankind. If I am having a heart attack, I do not want you waving a bundle of leeks over my head. At that particular moment, I would appreciate it very much if you would get me to a medical doctor. You can shake the leeks later.

On the other hand, we do not run to the doctor for every cut and sniffle. For the little things, we rely on either over-the-counter drugs or home remedies, and this is often where some wortcunning becomes applicable.

When I say "modern anatomical medicine," I mean just that. Anatomical medicine is not particularly "Western," regardless of what you may hear people say. I can assure you that there are doctors in Kyoto and Seoul who are well trained in modern anatomical medicine. Traditional Western medicine, much like traditional Chinese medicine, was based on elemental theory, and it made extensive use of diet, massage, and herbs. Definitions of health and healing were based on life processes rather than on body parts. Not that there is anything wrong with medicine based on body parts—as I have said, it has been a great boon to mankind. But this was not a traditional approach in either Europe or Asia.

To be honest, we do not know that much about how the pre-Christian Anglo-Saxons used herbs. Most of our information was recorded during the medieval period, after the English people had turned away from their gods. But I do not see that this really matters, because wortcunning is not a specifically religious activity. By the Middle Ages, English healers had adopted the elemental theory developed in southern Europe by scientists like Hippocrates and Aristotle. Elemental theory was a cornerstone of Western healing for nearly two thousand years. It was the most effective approach to healing in its time. It would have inevitably become part of Anglo-Saxon culture even in the absence of Christianity. In fact, the only actual spiritual shift that occurred in the practice of wortcunning was the prayers that became directed to the Christ and his saints, rather than to Woden and Sunne and Frige.

Elemental theory, in Europe at least, assumes that every substance in the universe has an underlying nature defined by temperature and humidity. That is, everything is either warm or cool, and either moist or dry, in varying degrees. These qualities are described in "elemental" terms of earth (cool/dry), water (cool/moist), air (warm/moist), and fire (warm/dry). Hippocrates, who became known as the father of medicine, applied this model to health and the human body with his theory of humors. A humor is essentially one of the four elements, but specifically in relation to the human body. These four humors are black bile (earth), phlegm (water), blood (air), and yellow bile (fire). When the humors are in balance, the body is in a state of health.

The Chinese developed a very similar theory, but in traditional Chinese medicine there are five elements. Four of these correspond with the four European elements described above. The Chinese images for these are metal (corresponding with earth), water, wood (corresponding with air), and fire. The fifth Chinese element is soil, and one of its functions is to balance or help regulate the other four. As with the European model, the Chinese elements relate not only to the human body but to everything in the universe.

European philosophers also eventually recognized a fifth element, which they called ether. But this development evolved after the theory of humors, and the Hippocratic model was so successful that the four-element model remained in place in traditional European medicine. The physician Galen later defined the ideal human condition as a slight excess of blood. That is, a slightly warm and moist condition.

In traditional Western healing, any chronic, significant imbalance was considered unhealthy, but the ailments that most often bother us tend to be cold conditions. And so today we say, "I've caught a cold," an expression that we apply indiscriminately to almost any generic, yucky feeling of disease. We do not care what kind of virus may be responsible. It is a cold. We know what a cold condition feels like, and the only thing that really matters is that we get over it.

Mental disease is also very often a cold condition. When we say that we are feeling melancholy, what we are saying, quite literally, is that we have an excess of black bile. That is what the Greek words *melan khole* mean, "black bile," the condition of being cold and dry.

It should come as no surprise, then, that the herbs most often used for healing these cold conditions tend to be "hot" herbs, associated with the element of fire. Nor should it come as a surprise that many of the herbs we use to season our foods, in European cooking, are herbs associated with fire. We constantly prepare our meals using herbs that fight pernicious cold conditions. This is because wortcunning does not treat food and medicine as two different things. After all, there is no point in sipping at a little cup of herbal tea if you are going to turn around and eat a hefty dinner seasoned with herbs that will counteract whatever it was you brewed in that cup. Over countless generations, we have accustomed ourselves to prefer the taste of herbs that keep us healthy.

In northern Europe, the hottest, most fiery plants were the alliums: onions, leeks, and garlic. These plants were known to be effective in combating pernicious cold conditions. Unlike leafy herbs, alliums are valued primarily for their thick, aromatic bulbs or stalks. The Anglo-Saxons recognized that these herbs were all related to each other. Our word *garlic*, in fact, is just Old English for "spear leek," meaning an exceptionally potent leek. Garlic was believed to be a protection against all diseases, including those caused by harmful wights. In the popular imagination, we still envision it as a substance that repels vampires!

The alliums we don't see used by the Anglo-Saxons are chives, but that's because these are Asian in origin. It was Marco Polo who first introduced chives into Europe. Chives do not form bulbs of any importance. Instead, their slender, cylindrical leaves have a mild onion flavor, as well as the magical or medicinal qualities shared by all of the alliums.

Alliums have mild antibiotic properties, and this pharmaceutical quality is utilized with the onions and garlic that inevitably find their way into any pot of homemade chicken soup. You didn't really think it was the noodles that made you feel better, did you?

The herb rosemary arrived in Britain with the Roman legions, where it eventually found a place in Anglo-Saxon culture. This is another herb considered to be hot and dry, another herb of fire. Rosemary was once burned in sick chambers to repel hostile spirits and purify the area. It also strengthens the *myne*, the part of your "soul" that retains memories and feelings. Young lovers used to give the objects of their affection bouquets including a few sprigs of rosemary "for remembrance," and brides often carried or wore rosemary wreaths tied with ribbons. This same property, remembrance, is why rosemary was also used in funeral wreaths.

As a memory herb, rosemary can be particularly helpful for students. Sprigs of the herb can be sewn into a sachet or just tucked into a small pouch. Rosemary under the pillow is said to prevent nightmares. The infusion ("tea") is also a good antiseptic, and can be used as a gargle or mouthwash.

Moving away from the spice cabinet, the herb chamomile, most often valued today as an herbal tea, was known to the Anglo-Saxons as "sweet leaf" because of its apple-scented leaves. The leaves retain their scent when dried, and they can be used in potpourri or sachets. Chamomile placed inside a pillow can help insomnia.

Comfrey was once known as bruisewort. Need I say more? It has been grown in many countries, both as fodder for animals and as food for human beings, but it is now believed to be dangerous if taken internally. Fortunately bruises are generally an external phenomenon. The fresh leaves can be applied as a poultice to relieve sore joints and sprains. The poultice may also be applied to reduce swelling around a fracture (assuming, of course, that you have already gone to the doctor and had the fracture properly set). These herbs are effective, but they are not a substitute for competent medical attention.

There are many books published featuring detailed information about herbs. Most of these focus entirely on pharmaceutical herbal remedies, but some also include interesting folklore about the plants.

Rune Magic

No book on Anglo-Saxon spirituality would be complete without at least some mention of the runes. Quite a few books about runes have been published over the years, but very little has been said specifically about the Anglo-Saxon runes, known also as the Futhorc. I will touch on a few points here that I think are important for the Saxon Pagan to understand.

One misperception to put aside is that there is a single set of "the" runes. The engraved stones or baked pottery often sold as "the" runes are a set known as the Elder Futhark. There is also a set of Norse runes known as the Younger Futhark, and still another set of English runes, which, as I have said, are called the Futhorc. These latter two sets bear a resemblance to the first, but they are distinctly different and are described by their own respective Rune Poems.

The Rune Poems give us some insight as to the esoteric meanings ascribed to the Futhorc and the Younger Futhark. Unfortunately there is no surviving poem or other lore for the Elder Futhark. The meanings now attributed to the Elder Futhark are based on those of similar runes in the later Norse and English runic alphabets.

If you decide to study the runes, you will very soon encounter an odd and incorrect idea about something called the "blank rune." This idea is built on the misperception that the runes are the little rocks or chips that the symbols are engraved into. They are not. The runes are the symbols themselves. If you do not have a symbol, you do not have a rune. To speak of the "blank rune" is like referring to the space bar on your keyboard as the twenty-seventh letter of the alphabet. The Elder Futhark, the rune set described in almost every rune book available today, consists of exactly twenty-four runes. That twenty-fifth "rune" in the set you purchased is just a rock.

Hang on to that blank rock, though. It will come in handy when you lose one of your runes, which is very likely to happen if you use them frequently. At that point you can paint the missing symbol on your "blank rune" and have a complete set of the Elder Futhark again.

Some will argue that people have been successfully using the "blank rune" ever since the concept was introduced to the public in the early 1980s. I would not presume to dispute this. Sortilege (fortunetelling by drawing random lots) is a venerable practice in almost all Pagan cultures. But it is not *rúncræft*. If you are going to make up something like the "blank rune," why bother with the deeper mysteries of the runes at all? Why not just make up all of your symbols? Wouldn't using a dollar sign to represent prosperity, or a heart to represent love, be easier than trying to understand the meaning of arcane symbols like *feoh*, *gyfu*, or *sigel*?

I am not being entirely sarcastic here. I would never, myself, have bothered with the runes if sortilege was all I was interested in. It would make far more sense to use something like the tarot, with illustrations painted on each card to let you know exactly what that card is supposed to represent. It would also be much simpler to use a home-brewed system with symbols similar to those I described above. You know instantly what the dollar sign is supposed to represent. You could use an exclamation point as a symbol for an unexpected factor, a smiley face for a general positive outcome, or an arrow to suggest activity or movement. And you would save yourself endless hours of study, because these are symbols you are already familiar with.

So why study the runes? Because they embody the mysteries of Saxon spirituality. This brings us to another misperception. You may hear that *feoh* means "money," or that *nied* means "necessity," but no rune has any one simple meaning like this. Each rune is a full mystery, with layers of revelation and depth that you will not find in your home-brewed set of symbols. You can study the runes for a lifetime and never stop learning more about, and from, them.

If this is not your goal, then I do not think you should waste your time with the runes. As with any other skill, rúncræft is not required for all Saxon Pagans. There is no law that says you have to know anything at all about runes.

Like the art of faring forth, runes can be either a means of divination or a means of working magic, or both. In the practice of magic, runes are carved to create talismans for various purposes. They are sometimes carved in a row, much like a script, and at other times they may be combined into "bindrunes," creating arcane symbols by superimposing the image of one rune over another.

The Younger Futhark is a shorter set of symbols than the Elder, with only sixteen runes. For some reason, many Ásatrúar (Icelandic Pagans) seem to prefer the Elder Futhark, but I've known a few who have made use of the runes associated with their own spiritual path. The Younger Futhark does not just have fewer symbols; the symbols it does have are defined by the Icelandic and

Norse Rune Poems, which do not always interpret a rune in the same way.

However, I am neither Norse nor Icelandic, so my interest is with the Futhorc. These runes are defined by the Anglo-Saxon Rune Poem, which describes no less than five more runes than are found in the Elder Futhark, thirteen more than in the Younger. Futhermore, there are an additional four Anglo-Saxon runes for which we have no record of their meaning. This makes a grand total of thirty-three runes in the Futhorc.

Don't let all of this confuse or discourage you. If you want to study the runes, go ahead and begin with the Elder Futhark. It is easier to get information about that, and you can always build on it later. All of the runes of the Elder Futhark are also found in the Futhorc, so you will do fine. You just won't be playing with a full deck, so to speak. After you have mastered the Elder Futhark, you can eventually go on to learn about the other runes specific to the Futhorc.

Trust me, if you open up that door you will still be learning more about these ancient, mysterious symbols thirty years from now.

Mead Made Simple

The myths passed down to us say that it was the god Woden who first gave us the runes. These same myths tell us that it was also Woden who gave us the drink known as mead. As the story goes, the first mead was brewed by dwarves (who are known for making the very best stuff, whether it is weaponry or jewelry or delicious beverages). This first batch of mead, so the story goes, fell into the hands of giants. Then Woden—a master shapeshifter—managed to steal it from them by changing into a snake and then into an eagle.

This is, of course, the abridged version. I have left out many details of the story. It is a Scandinavian tale, so there is a lot of blood and killing, which is sort of a trademark for Norse myths.

The important point of the story is that mead, the golden dwarf-brew, was a gift from the gods. Mead was the inspiration of the Saxon *scop* (pronounced "shope"), who entertained with song and poetry. This drink of fermented honey was given to newlyweds to ensure that their first month of marriage, their honey-moon, would be a sensuous and memorable experience. Treaties were bound, pacts were sealed, and oaths were sworn over horns brimming with the drink. Throughout northern Europe, mead truly was the nectar of the gods. Mead inspires vision, and eases sorrow.

In its most basic definition, mead is a fermented drink made of honey, water, and some kind of yeast. Essentially it is a honey wine. Although it is entirely possible to be a Saxon Pagan and never touch a drop of the stuff, the role of mead in Anglo-Saxon spirituality, at least on some symbolic level, cannot be overemphasized. There are as many Old English words relating to mead as there are to magic. There was a word for the cup or horn that the mead was served from, and for the bench a man sat on while drinking from that cup. The Anglo-Saxons even had a word (*medustig*) for the path that led to the hall where mead was being served!

It is easy to brew mead, but brewing a "pure" mead with just honey and water can be tricky. And so other flavoring agents are often added to the mix, creating a wide variety of meads, each with its own name.

A *cyser* is a drink made of honey and apple juice. Of all the possible variants, I would rather brew a cyser than anything else. Apple juice is very forgiving. It is possible to brew a bad-tasting cyser, but this is still a good choice for the novice brewer. The apple juice tends to cover minor "off" flavors that may be acquired during the brewing process.

A drink made of honey and hops—or honey and malt— is referred to as a *braggot*. As you might expect, this variety of mead has a taste similar to that of a beer. A person who can brew a decent stout can usually make a palatable braggot as well. On the other hand, I have tasted a braggot that only good manners kept me from spitting back out.

Pyments are made of honey and grape juice. When made with red grapes, a pyment has the appearance of a wine. The honey, however, gives this drink its distinct flavor. In my opinion, pyments are much like braggots in that they can range from very good to awful.

When you hear people talk about a *melomel*, they mean a drink made from a combination of honey and any fruit. Well, any fruit other than apples or grapes, since those are used in cysers and pyments. Mulberries are also excluded from this category. A drink of honey and mulberries is called a *morat*. But when a drink is brewed from honey and any fruit other than apples, grapes, or mulberries, it's called a melomel. Are you confused yet?

If herbs or spices are added to a mead during the brewing process, it becomes a *metheglin*. The metheglin was originally a medicinal substance, essentially a variation of the herbal tincture. But somewhere along the road, people noticed that certain herbs and spices tasted pretty darn good in a base of fermented honey.

How about now? Confused?

Fortunately mead aficionados today usually bypass this linguistic maze and slap the generic word "mead" onto all of these drinks. So don't worry if you can't remember a cyser from a melomel, or a morat from a metheglin, because in all likelihood you will hear these various drinks described as apple meads, pear meads, mulberry meads, or vanilla meads rather than by their official names. The exception to this is the braggot, which I have never heard described as anything but a braggot.

On the other hand, if you can brew a really good braggot, you've earned the right to give it a fancy name.

We are talking about alcoholic drinks here, so let me quickly toss in a disclaimer. If you are not old enough to legally drink, then don't, okay? You may think that the law is terribly unfair, especially if you are only months away from your state's drinking age. I won't disagree with you. Most of our laws concerning alcohol in the United States are founded on a Puritan ethic. But it is the law. It is not necessary to drink alcohol to follow the path of a Saxon Pagan, and your breaking the law needlessly only gives the rest of us a bad name.

Likewise, if you are an adult and interested in brewing your own mead, investigate your local laws first. Throughout most of the United States, if it is legal for adults to purchase commercially produced alcohol, it is also legal to brew nondistilled drinks (mead, wine, or beer) for your own use. Nevertheless, there are inevitably some restrictions to distinguish the hobby brewer from the professional distributor. Typically there will be a limit on how much you can legally brew in a calendar year. This quantity is usually way more than any normal person can possibly consume. At least not if that person is going to simultaneously hold down a job or function in any coherent way. Nevertheless, it is a good idea to familiarize yourself with the law, and with how much mead you can legally produce.

At one time, Pagan people throughout the United States brewed their own mead because it was next to impossible to obtain commercially. Today it is often available in wine and liquor stores, but many Pagans still prefer to make their own. Why? One reason is the lack of variety. Although you can often find a generic honey mead at your local wine store, you will not find the seemingly endless diversity of melomels, cysers, and metheglins that can be brewed at home. And as a home brewer, you can adapt any of these to suit your own preferences. You can make your mead sweet or dry, use light honey or dark amber honey, experiment with different strains of yeast, and create something unique and personal.

This last factor—the personal quality—is the real reason so many Saxon Pagans brew their own mead. Much of it will eventually be poured out for the gods and spirits in húsles. And as with any other gift, something you made yourself, investing your heart and effort into it, is much more dear and meaningful than a similar but mass-produced item.

When people *don't* brew their own mead, it is often for the wrong reasons. They may have been led to believe that it is a difficult process, or that they need a lot of expensive equipment and supplies to get started. Some of this may be their own imagining, but there are a number of brew-snobs who seem to delight in nurturing and maintaining this illusion.

I can assure you that the early Anglo-Saxons did not have hydrometers, thermometers, aeration stones, or fancy champagne yeasts. They did not always have the very best honey. The honey they used came from their own hives, varying greatly in both quantity and quality from one year to the next. They did not use refractometers or acid-testing kits. So don't believe the brew-snobs when they try to tell you that you need all of this stuff. You don't.

There are references in the sagas to the Vikings (cousins to the Anglo-Saxons) drinking "frothing mead." Mead froths while it is still in the process of fermenting. That's right, the Vikings didn't even wait until their mead was finished!

Thirty years ago, I used to go to Pagan gatherings in the Ozark Mountains where home-brewed mead was passed around in ordinary plastic milk jugs. Most of the brewers' equipment came from their own kitchens, and they used whatever yeast and honey they could get their hands on. I have pleasant memories of sitting up late into the night, drinking this brew under a harvest moon. The drink was often a cyser, but melomels were common and sometimes the brew would be a plain honey mead. It was not the best mead ever produced. Sometimes the first cup had an "off" taste. But by the time I got around to my third cup, it was tasting mighty good.

Hillbilly Mead

If you are interested in brewing your own mead (and if it is legal for you to do so), give this method a try. Don't wait around until you have saved up enough cash to buy your own version of an alchemist's laboratory. It is not as if you are only going to have one chance in life to brew the perfect batch of mead. If you enjoy doing this and decide that you want to "upgrade" your equipment, you can always do that later.

You will need a large pot, a long-handled stirring spoon, two one-gallon jugs (or equivalent), two corks or caps for the jugs, two balloons, and a needle. Glass or ceramic jugs are preferable, but plastic milk jugs will work in a pinch. The important thing is that all of your equipment—the jugs, the pot, the spoon, and the corks—be thoroughly cleaned. The brew-snobs will tell you that everything has to be sterile, but don't let this intimidate you. Home brewers make their mead in their kitchens, not in hospital surgeries. When you hear someone say that you need to sterilize your equipment, they just mean that you need to make sure it is very, very clean.

You will also need two pounds of honey and some yeast. If you live near a winemaking store, go ahead and buy a packet of sweet or dry mead yeast. Otherwise any yeast, even ordinary baking yeast, will work. It won't work as well, but it will work.

Bring three quarts of water to a boil in your pot for ten minutes, and then remove this from the heat and slowly stir in your honey. You don't want to boil the mixture itself, as this breaks down the flavor of the honey. If you want this to be a cyser, substitute six cups of apple juice for half of the water. I would recommend this, at least for your first batch of mead. I have had much better luck with cysers than with straight honey meads. But if you want to keep things simple, go ahead and stick with the water and honey mix.

Stir until the honey has completely dissolved. If you are feeling creative, this is the time to add any fruits (for a melomel) or spices (for a metheglin). A pound of fruit should be sufficient if you want to try a melomel. For a metheglin, begin with just a small quantity of spice. You can always add more later to suit your taste.

After your honey has dissolved, let the mixture cool until it returns to room temperature. Remembering that you are aiming for conditions bearing a vague resemblance to sterility, cover the pot while it cools. Carefully touch the outside of the pot periodically to determine how warm it is.

When the honey and water has cooled, add your yeast and stir this in. One packet of yeast is plenty, regardless of whether you are using an actual mead yeast or ordinary baking yeast. Now pour the mixture into your two jugs, dividing it evenly. If money is burning holes in your pocket, you can go back down to the winemaking store and buy a large five-gallon jug, often called a carboy, but this is another item that falls into the "luxury" category. Small one-gallon jugs will work just fine for brewing a small quantity of mead like this. While pouring the mixture, let it splash down into the jugs. This aerates the liquid, which will provide the yeast cells with more oxygen. Each jug should be a little over half full. You don't want them any more full than this because, if you have done everything right, the whole mess is going to start fermenting during the next few days.

If you are experimenting with a melomel, be sure to chop your fruit into fine pieces that you can later remove from the jug. Your fruit will swell slightly as it soaks in the liquid. More advanced mead making involves the use of a fermentation pail for the initial fermenting, so the size of the fruit pieces is not so much of a concern.

Drop a tea bag into each jug to add tannin. This is another easy but modern innovation. Tea was not introduced into England until the seventeenth century. It was still a relatively new fad among the English when we Americans had our falling-out with King George.

Using your needle, prick three holes in both of the balloons. Then put a balloon over each of the jugs. These balloons will allow carbon dioxide from the fermentation to escape while keeping out nasty bacteria that can turn your mead into vinegar. I have found it helpful to secure the balloons with heavy rubber bands around the neck of the jug.

The brew-snobs will tell you that you absolutely cannot brew a drinkable mead without commercially manufactured airlocks. If you are spending money on a carboy and mead yeast, you might as well pick up a couple of these little plastic devices while you are at the winemaking store, but I have never heard of anyone finding an airlock in an ancient Anglo-Saxon burial mound. I don't think they even had plastic back then. What I do know is that many people have successfully used balloons to protect their brew while making mead. I suspect the Anglo-Saxons didn't have party balloons either, but these are readily available and cheap, and you really just need something to keep bacteria out of your mead.

Keep the mead in a location where it will remain at room temperature and out of direct sunlight. Regardless of what the Vikings did, don't drink your mead while it is still fermenting. This is the twenty-first century, after all. Show some restraint. Let the fermentation process completely finish. This should take a few weeks. If you used a transparent jug, you can tell because no more bubbles will form on the sides. At this point, you can remove the balloons and seal the jugs with corks or caps. But don't do this while the brew is still fermenting, or it can and very likely will explode.

———

That is all there is to making a batch of hillbilly mead. There are countless things you can do to improve this procedure. I recommend siphoning your mead into new, clean jugs before corking it, in order to separate the fermented liquid from the sediment of dead yeast cells that will be left behind. You will see this sediment easily if your jugs are transparent. The dead yeast looks like an accumulation of dirt at the bottom of the jug. These dead cells always give your mead an "off" flavor, so siphoning the liquid into a new jug—a process called "racking"—will inevitably improve the final product. But even this is not strictly necessary, especially if you will be using the mead soon.

What if your mead goes bad? This is going to happen sometimes, no matter what kind of yeast you use or how much you spend on glassware and equipment.

It should go without saying that bad mead is never offered to the gods and spirits. This does not mean that everything you offer at a húsel needs to be an award-winning brew. But if you wouldn't drink it yourself, the gods certainly don't want the stuff. Sometimes it just needs to age more. I came very close once to pouring an entire carboy of mead down the drain, but instead I decided to let it sit a little longer. And then, quite by accident, I forgot about it. About nine months later I remembered that I had a big bottle of mead in the back room. By then the taste had mellowed, and it turned out to be one of the better batches I have made.

But sometimes you find yourself with something that is completely, undeniably undrinkable. Letting it age did not help at all. It is not something you would present to the gods or to your ancestors. Nevertheless, it may still be useful in its own way as a cooking mead.

Have you ever tasted cooking sherry? Nasty stuff. But the manufacturer didn't intend you to drink it out of the bottle. (And maybe you should look into an AA meeting if you are doing something like that.) When mead goes bad, as often as not, it turns to vinegar. And this honey vinegar can be great to cook with. It makes a very nice marinade for beef or pork or chicken. I hardly ever throw out a batch of mead anymore, even if it is not something I want to drink.

Pot roast is improved greatly when you cook it in "bad" mead. And by bad, keep in mind that I mean mead that has turned into a honey vinegar. If you have somehow managed to grow fuzz on top of your brew, throw it away. Use common sense.

Mead Pot Roast

There is nothing particularly religious about this, but it makes a great dinner after you and your friends have held a húsel. And it is a good use for the batch of mead that didn't turn out right. Even if you have a good mead, you can save the dregs—the remaining part with its dead yeast cells—to use in this simple recipe.

Roll a chuck roast in flour. Heat a few tablespoons of oil in a skillet and brown the meat on all sides. Transfer the roast to a large pot, add a full cup of mead, and season the meat with a little salt, pepper, and thyme. Cover this and let it simmer for about an hour.

Now chop up a couple of white potatoes and three carrots. The pieces do not have to be particularly small. About two inches across is fine. Add the vegetables to the pot, cover it again and let it cook for another forty-five minutes or so. I usually add a little more mead, perhaps half a cup, when I add the vegetables.

After the vegetables are tender, remove them and the roast and put them on a separate plate. Then make a gravy from the remaining juices.

This usually comes out delicious, and people who have never cooked with mead will wonder why your pot roast has such a wonderful flavor. After you have made a mead pot roast, you may also want to experiment with chicken and pork recipes.

———

Brewing is like magic in that it is a skill, and not everyone will have a talent for it. There is no Saxon law, no thew nor custom, that says you have to brew mead if you want to worship the gods. If brewing is not your thing, just pick up a bottle of mead at your local liquor or wine store. And if they don't have it, ask if they will order some for you. Specialty stores are often willing and happy to expand their inventory if they know there is a market for a certain product.

Some people, of course, should not be handling any kind of alcohol. As mentioned earlier, if it is illegal for you to drink or handle mead, then don't. And obviously if you have a problem with alcoholism, you should avoid mead and any other fermented beverage. If this is your situation, you have two alternatives. The first is to use some form of fruit juice. I think apple juice is best, but that is just my personal taste. In appearance, apple juice resembles a honey mead, and of course it is a component of any cyser.

Your second option is to make a nonfermented mead. Think of it as a frothing mead before the frothing starts. This is basically a mix of water and honey. Heat water and blend in honey as described in the process above. Do not add any yeast. And do not assume that the stuff will not ferment just because you did not add yeast. Undiluted honey doesn't ferment, because it has a low water content. Bees are very smart in that way. They evaporate their honey until it reaches a point where it will not ferment.

But you have just added a lot of water back into the honey, so try to be as smart as a bee. Do not let this mixture sit around very long, and if it must set more than a few hours, be sure to refrigerate it.

Ideally, though, there is nothing quite like the real thing. Whether you buy it at the store or brew your own unique batch, the gods and ancestors and elves always appreciate an offering of good, flavorful mead.

Gathering at the Hearth

It is entirely possible to worship the gods on your own. Neither Woden nor Frige nor Thunor will object if you approach your wéofod alone. But most Saxon Pagans enjoy group worship, and there are some who say that you cannot fully appreciate our path without including this communal aspect. I don't know if I would go that far, but participation in a Saxon *inhíred* (pronounced "in-HEAR-ed") can certainly enhance your spirituality.

Group worship can be a powerful experience. Most contemporary Pagan religions have some form of group worship. The Hellenic Pagan has his demos, the Ásatrúar his kindred, the Wiccan his coven. The Saxon Pagan has his inhíred.

In Old English the word *inhíred* means a household or family. And that pretty much sums up what the word means to Saxon Pagans today. Some *inhírdas* are families in a very "traditional," Republican sense. Acstead Inhíred, in the Midwestern United States, consists of one nuclear family. Dad, mom, and offspring. They have no members outside of their immediate family and, at least at the time I am writing this, they are perfectly content to keep things that way.

Inhíred is only one word that Saxon groups use. A group might refer to itself as a *mót* or a *hearth*, or by some other name. To avoid confusion, we will use *inhíred* throughout this chapter.

Historically one's *híredmenn* were almost always blood relatives. But ours is a living religion, not a historic re-enactment society. Many of us today are separated from our blood kin, by physical distance if nothing else. Because of work, school, love, and other factors, we may find ourselves hundreds, perhaps thousands, of miles away from any of our blood relatives.

There are also other reasons why we may find ourselves estranged from our blood kin. Although polytheist faiths accept and respect other paths, there are other religions that are not quite so enlightened. Many Saxon Pagans have found themselves ostracized by their families because they chose to follow the old gods. As sad and frustrating as this can be, it is a fact of life.

Even if this does not occur, blood kin (unless you were born into our religion) have their own paths to follow. Most of us today were raised in another faith. And since our blood relatives usually do not share our religion, the Saxon inhíred will often be a family of choice. While this is, for the most part, a modern innovation, it is not without historical precedent. The early Anglo-Saxons were known to shift tribal and familial allegiance through an exchange of oaths. In a similar way, modern Saxons create inhírdas through an exchange of oaths with their fellow híredmenn. In this way, we build a sense of community within our own culture.

On a purely psychological level, membership in an inhíred can be an extremely rewarding experience. Another difference we see in the twenty-first century is the vast size of the greater society we all live in. This in itself can leave us with a feeling of isolation. People today often search for some sense of identity. This is the underlying reason why many people become so passionate about a sports team. Professional sports teams consist of athletes who are brought in from across the nation to play a game for a specific city team. They are rarely natives of the city they supposedly represent, nor are they related to their fans in any way. But these athletes and the games they play give sports fans a sense of identity. The fans invest their emotions in their local team much in the same way that the early Anglo-Saxons felt about their small kingdoms.

This same need for a sense of identity is why some people join gangs or secret societies. The quest for a sense of place and purpose is quite natural, but it sometimes manifests in ways that can only be described as unhealthy.

The inhíred can provide a more positive sense of identity for the Saxon Pagan. Híredmenn share in what amounts to a small tribe of like-minded people who they can trust and confide in. Belonging to an inhíred connects you with people who share your interest in and love of the old gods. All of your fellow híredmenn can benefit by taking advantage of each others' talents. One person may lead the monthly húsles, while another serves as the community drýmann. If one member can play a guitar or recorder, the entire group can enjoy live music during its rites. A híredmann might be an exceptional cook or have a talent for brewing delicious meads.

As I've mentioned, some inhírdas are composed entirely of blood relatives, while others are families of choice. In the latter case, some are nearly as communal as a family of blood relatives, spending most of their time together, while other inhírdas may only meet once or twice a month. Some have very little structure. Some are as hierarchical and ritualized as a Masonic lodge.

I personally favor less structure. When we keep in mind that the inhíred is a Saxon household, the need for rank and title seems unnecessary to me. Saxon Pagans find it helpful to use certain labels to describe various offices within the inhíred, but I think this works better when we treat these labels as functional rather than titular. The label should describe what a person does, not who he is.

The leader of a Saxon inhíred is often called the *ealdor*, the Old English word for "elder" or "head of the family." The ealdor is usually one of the oldest members, but this is specifically in relationship to the other híredmenn. If everyone in the inhíred is a young adult, the ealdor could be a young person in his twenties! Often, but not always, the ealdor will be the person who initially organized the inhíred. In some inhírdas the ealdor is called the *thyle* ("THEUL-eh"), meaning the spokesperson for the group. Whatever this person is called, this is who the other híredmenn look to for leadership. This is not a title that can be worn like a crown. To be the ealdor of an inhíred is to be in a position of service. Ealdors lead their groups not because they are superior to the other híredmenn, but because they are willing and capable of doing the work.

A lot of potential problems disappear when the position of the ealdor is treated as functional rather than titular. Unfortunately, ealdors will occasionally attempt to set themselves up as autocrats, presuming to have some authority that exists only in their own imagination. Do not make this mistake if you should find yourself serving as the ealdor of your inhíred. Your authority really extends only as far as your fellow híredmenn are willing to give you their respect and loyalty.

In most inhírdas, the adult members are referred to as *gesithas* ("YES-sith-es"). This word means "companions." All gesithas within the inhíred are equals, regardless of whether or not they hold some other functional position within the group. The ealdor is also a gesith, a leader among peers.

In larger groups, ealdors often need to delegate tasks. They may designate one of their gesithas as a *thegn* (pronounced "thane"). This basically means an attendant or servant. The thegn is responsible for whatever duties the ealdor has delegated. Thegnes may be responsible for keeping the group's ritual gear, or for notifying everyone when the next húsel will be held. A large inhíred may have several thegnes with different responsibilities.

If the inhíred is fortunate enough to have a musician among its members, that person might be designated as the scop. As with the other functional positions, a scop serves the other híredmenn, in this case by providing music during, before, or after a rite.

Keep in mind that every gesith is a híredmann, but a híredmann is not necessarily a gesith. The gesithas are the companions—the full members—of the group. *Híredmann* is a more general word that also includes people who are attached to the household in some way but may have no obligation or responsibility to it. This includes children. Very often it may include the spouse of a gesith who follows a different faith but nevertheless accepts a place of kinship within the inhíred.

The word *híredmann* also describes the person who is considering full membership in the group, but has not yet made that commitment. Very few inhírdas will accept a new member until that person has met with the group consistently for a period of time. A year's probation is typical. The prospective member can usually participate in everything the group is doing, and is indistinguishable from any gesith. This individual is in many ways a functional member of the inhíred, and yet everyone is aware that either side can call off the engagement at a moment's notice.

At the end of the year, or however long the wait may be, the new híredmann may give an oath binding him to the group, and at that time he becomes a gesith. He is then a companion, or peer, equal to his fellows.

When an inhíred accepts a new gesith, the entire group takes on this person's orlay as part of their own. This is that "acquired orlay" we discussed in the fourth chapter. Oathing to an inhíred is very much a marriage of spirit, and it should be approached with the same caution and consideration as any other marriage. Restraint in oathing to an inhíred can be difficult for the Saxon Pagan, as our culture, modeled on the Old English construct of the village, is inherently tribal. Nevertheless, oathing to the wrong group will prove to be more of a burden than a joy.

The Gesithscipe Oath

It is the ealdor of the inhíred who formally accepts the new gesith's oath, known as the *gesithscipe oath*. But when the position of ealdor is functional rather than titular, the oath is to the inhíred itself, and not to any individual person. This is a very important distinction. The path that I follow is not a path of subservience. The ealdor accepts the oath on behalf of the entire inhíred. In this way, the ealdor is indeed the thyle, or spokesperson, for the other gesithas.

Before such an oath is given or accepted, all parties involved should be fully aware of its implications. The inhíred is not a simple social club. The potential gesith is essentially swearing "blood brotherhood" with everyone in the group. Everyone. If there is even one person in the inhíred who the new member does not feel a connection with, or vice versa, the oath should be postponed and reconsidered. It should go without saying that none of the gesithas should feel pressured in any way to accept the new member, nor should the new member feel pressured to join the group. Any sense of pressure, real or imagined, is a clear sign that the oath should be reconsidered.

There is no shame in not being accepted into an inhíred. It does not mean you "aren't right." It only means you were not right for that particular group. Or perhaps the group recognized that they were not right for you. Respect their decision and do not take it as a personal criticism.

If everyone does want to go ahead with the oath, this is usually done just before the offerings are made during a group húsel, which is described later in this chapter. Although the entire inhíred doesn't need to attend, all of the gesithas—the oathed members—should be present. Otherwise it is a little like getting married while the groom has gone fishing. The difference is that here there may be quite a few "grooms," and it may be impossible to get all of them together for the next húsel, and there may be a time element involved for one reason or another. The ealdor accepts the oath on behalf of the inhíred, so it is possible to do this without everyone present. Ideally, however, all of the gesithas should witness the oath.

The oath is given over a horn, or cup, filled with mead. This is one time when I think the use of real mead is important. I would rather see this oath given with a horn of nonfermented mead, a mix of water and honey, than something like wine or beer. And my first preference, of course, would be a fermented mead, either home-brewed or purchased from a commercial supplier. The ancient Anglo-Saxons swore oaths over mead, and at this time, more than almost any other, the inhíred is connecting with that ancestral culture on a spiritual level.

The híredmann should stand before the ealdor and say,

If you see me as worthy, I would be known as a gesith of [name of inhíred]. *I will give worship to the gods of the Anglish, and no other gods will I honor above them. I will hold the folk of* [name of inhíred] *as my own brothers and sisters, taking their doom and upholding their honor as my own. If ever I cannot in good faith hold to this, I will ask release from my oath or be forever foresworn. This I swear, in the names of Tiw and Thunor.*

"Doom," as we use it here, is from the Old English *dóm*, which is often translated as "judgment," but the word is more complex than that. *Doom* refers both to a person's destiny and state of being. Here it is similar to the idea of "for richer or poorer."

Hopefully, if things have progressed this far, the ealdor will accept the oath. He should raise the horn or cup and say,

You have shown yourself to be worthy, and your words are well spoken. Those who take upon themselves the doom of [name of inhíred] *shall ever have the love of* [name of inhíred].

The ealdor now takes a sip from the horn and says,

If you would be a gesith of [name of inhíred]*, drink of the mead of inspiration and be joined to us, blood to blood.*

Now the ealdor passes the horn to a gesith other than the oathing híredmann. The gesith who accepts the horn takes a sip. He may, if he wishes, say something personal here, but he ends his words with "blood to blood" and passes the horn on to another gesith. When all of the gesithas have supped from the horn, the last passes it to the oathing híredmann.

The híredmann may want to say something more now, perhaps expressing appreciation or affection, or making a personal promise of some kind. He then completes the round of oaths by repeating the words "blood to blood" and drinking from the horn. He is now a gesith, or companion of the inhíred.

———

And now everyone lives happily ever after, right? Well, maybe that happens somewhere on the Planet of Eternal Sunshine, but in the real world even the best-planned unions can sometimes end in divorce. This is true for híredmenn as much as for any other form of partnership. The commitment of a gesith should never be taken up frivolously. It should be sincere. But even with complete sincerity, even when all parties treat each other with honor and respect, it happens occasionally that a gesith must part ways with the inhíred.

The reason may not even be a bad thing. It may be that the gesith has been offered a fantastic job opportunity in another city hundreds of miles away. If he moves, he will undoubtedly still be "family"—a híredmann—but he will no longer be able to meet with the group on a regular basis. Thus he can no longer continue to serve as a full, functional member of the inhíred.

As given, the wording of the gesithscipe oath allows a gesith to part company when and if the time comes that he must do so. This is intentional. The gesith has promised to remain true to his oath until he "asks release." He must go to the ealdor—who may be either the person who accepted his oath, or the inhíred's current ealdor—and ask to be released from his vows. That is all he has to do. It is not the ealdor's place to decide whether or not to allow this. If the gesith has come forward to end the arrangement honorably, he has the right to do so.

By the same token, if the ealdor has determined that the inhíred can no longer embrace the gesith, he must let this be known. If the ealdor has any honor, he will make every effort to notify the (former) gesith. But if the ealdor ends the arrangement, there is no debate.

This may seem overly simplistic, but there is a fail-safe built into the commitment between a gesith and the inhíred. Gesithas worth their salt are not going to leave their inhírdas over some petty disagreement. Once gesithas leave, it is highly unlikely that they will ever be accepted back again. The exception being, of course, if they left because of conditions beyond their control, as in the example of somebody who had to move to follow a career. More often than not, however, if gesithas leave a group, it is because of "irreconcilable differences." If they leave for petty reasons, then their former híredmenn are probably better off without them anyway. Who would want to weave their orlay with those who storm off whenever things are not going their way?

Likewise, worthy ealdors only release gesithas from their oaths after all other avenues have been explored. The fail-safe here is that ealdors who dismisses gesithas because of a harsh word or personal disagreement, without the approval of the entire gesithscipe, will soon find themselves standing alone.

The Húsel

The third chapter of this book included a description of a private, personal húsel. This act, the offering of a sacrament, is the primary rite conducted by the inhíred. It is similar in many ways to an Ásatrú ritual known as a *blót*, and you may hear people refer to it by this name. However, while this word may have a different connotation in Old Norse, in Old English *blót* means "blood" and refers specifically to an animal sacrifice.

I would like to say a word here about animal sacrifice, and that word would be "don't." It is true that the Anglo-Saxons once sacrificed animals to our gods, but that doesn't mean it is appropriate for you to do so today. The Anglo-Saxons, like all pre-industrial peoples, butchered all of their own meat. It was a natural, ordinary part of their daily lives. Thus it was equally natural for them to include some ritual in this process to demonstrate their gratitude to the gods. They did not kill senselessly. The sacrifice was a ritual butchering, followed by offering a portion of the meat to the gods. It was more akin to a community barbecue than to a mysterious, occult ritual.

There is nothing especially manly about killing a defenseless animal. If you believe otherwise, please close this book, now, and try to find a psychologist or certified counselor who can help you.

The exceptions, of course, are those individuals who raise their own meat, for whom butchering is an integral and consistent part of their lifestyle. For the rest of us—the majority of us today—I believe it is inappropriate.

How often to hold a húsel is a decision for you and your fellow híredmenn to make. For most inhírdas this is a monthly event. The important thing is that you agree to some regular duration and keep this commitment, whether it is weekly, every other week, monthly, or whatever. I personally think anything less frequent than once a month is sort of weak as commitments go.

The Anglo-Saxons followed a lunar calendar, and in-hírdas today often meet at the full moon, but there is no hard and fast rule about this. If the lunar cycle gives you a sense of connection with the ancient Anglo-Saxons, that is all well and good. Like using a horn for libations, or wearing period clothing during worship, it can help you identify with the old ways. But holding your group húsles on the first Saturday of each month works equally well. In our contemporary culture, in fact, an arrangement like this is preferable when híredmenn would otherwise miss gatherings due to work or other commitments. As an alternative, your inhíred could compromise by meeting on the weekend following each full moon.

You should determine well in advance which god, goddess, or spirits the húsel will honor. This gives everyone a chance to prepare personal offerings if they choose to do so. If you will be making these offerings at a household wéofod, be sure to have some representation of the honored deity (the wéoh) at hand.

Begin the húsel by claiming or identifying the ritual area by carrying fire around its perimeter. A lantern or torch works better if you are meeting outdoors. Otherwise, inside, a candle will suffice just as well. As you process with the flame, say,

> *I carry fire around this holy stead, and ask all spirits to depart unless invited in. Thunor, ward this sacred place.*

Now offer some aromatic herbs or incense to the gods collectively. If you are indoors, burn the herbs or incense in your récelsfæt, the receptacle you keep on your wéofod for this purpose. Outdoors the herbs can be burned either in a récelsfæt or in some other contained fire. As you burn the herbs, say,

> *You who dwell in Osgeard, accept this gift and know that you are remembered by the folk of* [name of inhíred].

At this point the ealdor, or whoever is leading the rite, may speak briefly about the god or spirits who will be honored in the húsel. Even if everyone present is thoroughly familiar with Woden, it is a good idea to reflect on his nature for a few moments before making offerings to him. This "briefing" is especially important if any of the participants are *not* familiar with the deity or spirits in question.

These words are followed by the group offering. A libation, whether of mead or some other drink, works especially well for group offerings. The person leading the rite raises the horn (or chalice, or cup) and gives a prayer to the honored spirit. The wording of course depends on precisely who is being honored. If you are uncomfortable with extemporaneous speaking, write down what you want to say before the húsel begins. The offering prayer should express gratitude. A good prayer will be specific to the entity being honored.

Compare these two statements: "We give thanks, Woden, for all you've given us." And then this: "We give thanks, Woden, for the inspiration that drives us forward, for the wisdom to guide that inspiration, and for the courage to continue onward."

There is nothing inherently wrong with "for all you've given us," but that is something you could say to any god or goddess, or to the elves, or to your ancestors, for that matter. The second example makes it clear that you didn't just pull Woden's name out of a hat at the last minute.

After giving the prayer, the person leading the rite takes a sip from the horn and passes it to the next person. This next person may then say a few words if he feels moved to do so, drinks, and passes the horn. It isn't necessary to say anything, and I personally think silence is better than saying something that is obviously contrived. Or, if silence feels awkward, just say "thank you," drink, and pass the horn.

If the inhíred is using mead in the offering and you cannot or prefer not to imbibe for some reason, just touch the horn to your lips and pass it on.

Very often the horn (or cup or chalice) will be passed around three times. The first round is for the honored god or spirits of the occasion. If it is to Woden, for example, then everyone drinks to Woden. If it is to the elves, everyone drinks to the elves. The only variation here is in what each participant wishes to say (if anything) to the honored spirit or spirits.

The second round is to any god, goddess, or spirit. It is perfectly appropriate to raise the horn to Woden—or whoever the honored entity is—when it comes around a second time. But more often the horn will be raised to some other spirit. If the horn was raised to Woden in the first round, in the second it might be raised to Frige (his consort) or Thunor (his son). It might be raised to a spirit or wight who has no obvious relationship to the honored entity. The only restriction is that the horn be raised to an *Anglo-Saxon* spirit. It is inappropriate to honor the Greek goddess Athena or the Egyptian Horus in a Saxon húsel. This is not an offense so much to our gods as it is to these non-Saxon deities who are supposedly being "honored." They have their own rites, and should be worshipped accordingly. If you have a friend who is a vegetarian, do you think he will be pleased when you serve him prime rib? The húsel is the Saxon's prime rib. Save it for those spirits who will appreciate it.

The second round is specifically for spirits, gods, elves, or ancestors. You don't need to make a long speech, but since there is some question during this round as to whom you are raising the horn, some entity should be named even if you say no more than "to Woden" or "to our ancestors" as you drink or touch the horn to your lips.

During the third round, the horn can be raised to any wight, incarnate or discarnate. This includes the Saxon gods, the elves, the ancestors, or any living heroes or loved ones who you would like to remember and praise. The horn can be raised to any entity who has given meaning to your life.

After everyone has supped from the horn during its final round, whether it was passed just once or three times around, it is then returned to the person who gave the opening prayer. This person pours the remaining drink into the offering bowl, saying,

A gift for a gift. To the gods!

Or, where appropriate, "to the elves" or "to the ancestors." When you are meeting outdoors, the offering bowl is usually unnecessary. The libation is instead poured directly onto the earth.

Following this come the personal offerings. The ealdor, or whoever is leading the rite, will ask if anyone has brought a personal offering for the honored spirit. Those who have done so will come forward, one at a time. Depending on the nature of the offering, it may be put into the bowl or just set on the wéofod. The personal offerings are always to the spirit of the occasion, to whichever god or spirit was honored during the first passing of the horn or chalice. This is not the time to make offerings to other gods or goddesses. That's what the aromatic herbs were for.

A personal offering is, well, *personal*, so the wording that accompanies this must come from the heart. The form or nature of the offering will likewise vary. The effort you put into one of these gifts is more important than the nature of the gift itself. A flower you picked from a neighbor's garden or growing along the road is all but meaningless. The flower that you grew from seed, tending and nurturing it from the very beginning as a gift to Frige, is a much more worthy gift.

Nobody should feel obligated to bring a personal offering. These should always be sincere, heartfelt gifts. The earlier, group offering serves the entire inhíred. Anything more than this is a private exchange between the individual híredmann and his god, his ancestors, or the elves.

After any personal offerings have been brought forward, the húsel is brought to a close with a final prayer of thanks. This is presented by whoever gave the opening prayer.

You may have noticed that I made several references to "the ealdor, or whoever is leading the rite." The ritual leader often is the ealdor, but liturgical roles can be delegated however your group wishes. In some inhírdas, the same person may carry fire around the ritual area at every húsel. In others, this task may rotate from one híredmann to another.

————

Almost every Anglo-Saxon group defines itself as a family or tribe. For this reason, membership in an inhíred or kindred or mót is almost always restricted. You cannot simply sign up and join one of these groups as you would your local gardening club. On a national level, however, there are a few Pagan organizations with open memberships that can benefit the contemporary Saxon to some degree. Thanks to the Internet, it is now possible to join greater communities of like-minded individuals from all over the world.

The Troth (www.thetroth.org) is a more general Germanic organization whose members follow a variety of Heathen paths. They publish an entertaining and informative quarterly journal. The Troth has an international membership and accepts participants of any race, ethnic ancestry, or sexual orientation. Although not specifically Anglo-Saxon, this is another good resource for connecting with like-minded people who honor the gods of northern Europe. Not all groups affiliated with the Troth accept new members.

Ár nDraíocht Féin (www.adf.org) welcomes Pagans of any Indo-European faith. This is one of the larger and older Pagan organizations in the United States, and its members include Norse, Celtic, Roman, Hellenic, Slavic, and, yes, Saxon Pagans, among others. Defining itself as a druidic organization, ADF has developed a unique liturgy that provides a sort of "common language" for Pagans from these varied traditions. As with the Troth, the members of ADF enjoy access to various programs and publications. The disadvantage here is that it is highly unlikely that any extant local chapter (referred to as a *grove*) will be Anglo-Saxon, although Norse groves are not uncommon. However, many ADF groves accommodate more than one faith, honoring the gods of one pantheon at one rite, and the gods of a second pantheon at the next. If the local grove follows a Welsh tradition, its members may nevertheless be willing to hold a few Anglo-Saxon rites out of respect for your gods. If you accept this courtesy, be sure to extend the same respect to the Welsh deities in turn.

———

National organizations certainly have their place, but they are not true substitutes for the Saxon inhíred. Inhírdas, being spiritual households, do not restrict their gatherings to formal rituals. As any household might, they often meet at other times for purely social reasons—picnics, daytrips, dinners. When their blood kin live at a distance, híredmenn often gather together around the Thanksgiving table. Other secular holidays—New Year's Eve, Memorial Day, Independence Day, and so on—are also good times for inhírdas to get together.

And even in a purely religious context, most inhírdas meet not only for their normal húsles, but also to celebrate the holy feasts of the Saxon calendar.

Holy Tides

As I have said before, I consider my path to be a living religion, not a historic reenactment. Most Saxon Pagans define themselves as "reconstructionists," but it would be more accurate to say that what we have reconstructed is Anglo-Saxon spirituality as it would be practiced today, not as it was practiced in the very different, nondemocratic, pre-industrial England of fifteen centuries ago. Our reconstruction draws its inspiration from folklore dating to England's medieval period as much as from Anglo-Saxon poems, charms, and Old English linguistics.

What I am leading up to saying here is that the ancient Pagan traditions I am going to describe in this chapter are not necessarily all that ancient. You may hear people claim otherwise, but don't believe them. Yuletide customs, especially, are often characterized as ancient Pagan traditions. But the truth is, most of our pre-Christian European traditions have been lost in the mists of history. Very few customs can be reliably documented earlier than the sixteenth century. Almost everything we really know about the Pagan Saxon holy days has been preserved in Bede's writing, and he left us precious little.

Consider for a moment the ancient Pagan tradition of the Yule tree, or what our Christian cousins call the Christmas tree. You may have heard people say the custom of bringing an evergreen tree into the home can be traced back to pre-Christian Europe. Despite this romantic notion, Christmas trees were unknown anywhere in England until the eighteenth century, and at first even then were only a fashion among the nobility. Yuletide greenery of any kind can only be documented back to the sixth century, well into the Christian era. And this early greenery consisted not of trees, but of branches of rosemary, bay, and yew, as well as the traditional Victorian holly and ivy. To my knowledge, there is no real evidence of the early Anglo-Saxons bringing trees or any other greenery into their homes during the Yule season, and yet most Saxon Pagans today consider the Yule tree a valid and meaningful tradition. Why? Because it captures the spirit of the old traditions.

There may be no surviving evidence of the Anglo-Saxons bringing in Yuletide greenery, but there is also no evidence that they did *not* do something like this. We know that decorating the home with green boughs was an established solstice tradition in what is now northern Portugal at least as early as 575 CE. A local bishop there decried the "wicked" custom of decorating homes with "laurel and green branches," openly denouncing it as a Pagan celebration (Jones and Pennick 1995, 76). It is not unreasonable to suppose that the Anglo-Saxons, as well as other European peoples, may have had similar customs. And the tree itself is a beautiful reflection of our cosmology, a representation of the Eormensyl, the World Tree that connects our Middle Earth to the other realms.

This is what distinguishes reconstruction from re-enactment. Almost everything about our religion, to some degree or another, is a reconstruction. It is not necessarily exactly what the Anglo-Saxons did. It is what they may have done before the arrival of Augustine, or what they may have done if their indigenous culture had survived intact to this day.

Obviously this leaves a lot of room for interpretation. There is no "right" way to celebrate the holy tides, nor even an incontestable agreement as to what these days are. Most of us today observe eight holidays spaced roughly equidistant from each other throughout the calendar year.

If you are familiar with Wicca, these holidays are going to look more than a little familiar to you, and there is a reason for this. Wicca was cobbled together in the wake of the Second World War by Gerald Gardner, who assembled his new religion from a combination of English folklore and ceremonial magic. Two devastating wars with Germany had instilled an intense if understandable aversion to anything Germanic—including Anglo-Saxon culture—in the hearts of the English people. These feelings were so deep that the German shepherd dog, in England, was renamed the Alsatian. References to English ancestry became phrased in polite conversation as "Celtic," and today many people still believe that Gardner's holidays are Celtic in origin when, in fact, they are simply English. The Celts surely had at least some influence on their Saxon neighbors (and vice versa), but the holy tide of Yule (Old English: *Géola*), for example, is entirely Anglo-Saxon. In fact, none of the solstice or equinox celebrations have Celtic origins. Although the Celts celebrated the summer and winter solstice in later times, scholars believe they adopted these customs from their Germanic neighbors, not vice versa.

There is no one way these holidays must be observed, but most inhírdas will hold the usual húsel as a central feature of the celebration. Nevertheless, the húsel is not the holiday. During these holy tides we reach out not only to our gods, but to our families—whether families of blood or of choice—to celebrate life and health and kinship. Much like the secular holidays of Thanksgiving or Independence Day, these are times for híredmenn to spend the entire day together in celebration. And much like these secular holidays, each of our holy tides has its own traditions. They may not be ancient traditions, but, for Saxon Pagans, they connect us with the indigenous spiritual heritage of the early Anglo-Saxon people.

Ewemeolc

For some inexplicable reason, American calendars will often claim that March 21 is the day when "spring begins." This continues throughout the calendar year, announcing the beginning of summer in mid-June, the beginning of autumn in mid-September, and the beginning of winter in mid-December. These designations—all of them relatively new and uniquely American—perplex Europeans, who can't figure out why people in the United States think that summer begins in mid-summer. I personally believe it's a sad reflection of how disconnected we've become from the natural order of the world.

Spring begins not in March, but near the beginning of February during the holy tide of Ewemeolc ("YOO-meolk"). The date often given for this is February 2, but, like most of our holy tides, this is a seasonal observance rather than a specific calendar date. The word means "ewe's milk," and refers to the lactation of the ewes after the spring lambs have been born. And sheep are notorious for ignoring calendar dates. Historically, sheep in England were bred in late autumn, and would begin to drop their lambs at some time around the end of January. We may assume this event, quite by chance, actually did begin on February 2 once in a while.

Ewemeolc is arguably one of the holy tides that may have Celtic origins. The Scots, Welsh, and Irish all celebrated a holiday at this time of year. It is said that this Celtic holiday also celebrated the lactation of the ewes, but its central purpose was to honor the goddess Brigit or Brighid, who is not to my knowledge particularly associated with sheep at all. So was this connection with sheep a Celtic tradition or an Anglo-Saxon tradition? If both, did the Celts get the idea from the Saxons, or was it the other way around? However interesting such a debate might be for historians, for our purposes it really doesn't matter. Shepherding was not unique to either culture, and if both celebrated the lambing season, there is no reason to assume that this habit was derived from the Celts, or vice versa.

Daylight hours begin to increase just after the winter solstice, but this phenomenon becomes much more obvious by the end of January. For us today, longer days and the birthing of lambs may seem like minor events, but for the early Anglo-Saxons, this was nothing less than wondrous. Fresh food of any kind was scarce by this time of the year. Families were struggling to survive on old cabbages, root crops, and perhaps an occasional rabbit. The arrival of the lambs meant fresh milk and cheeses. More daylight meant that livestock could graze longer. Poultry would begin to produce more eggs.

I have heard it said that Pagans today should abandon these old agrarian associations for our holy tides and come up with something "more relevant." It seems so sad, to me, that anyone would think of the miracles that led up to their own existence as being unimportant or irrelevant. Today we can buy milk—although the selection is usually limited to cow's milk—at the supermarket throughout the year. But if it were not for the lactation of the ewes, it is unlikely that I would have been around to write this book, or that you would be around to read it. Our ancestors would have perished many centuries ago. This is what we celebrate each year at Ewemeolc—renewal and sustenance. In a very real way we are celebrating our very existence. If for no other reason, this is why it is still relevant to us as twenty-first-century Saxon Pagans.

Bede tells us that the Saxons baked cakes at this time of year and offered them to their gods. By "cakes" he didn't mean the frosting-covered sugar-bombs that we think of today. The cake would have been more like a bread. It has been suggested that these loaves or cakes were probably ploughed into the fields. Thus the cakes would have been offered not only to the gods in general, but also very specifically to the earth herself. Because of this, I honor Hertha each year during my Ewemeolc húsel. There seems to be a strong connection with the earth mother at this season. Long into the Christian era, the English agricultural season began in mid-January with a celebration known as Plough Monday, when the plough-share would actually be brought into the church to be blessed.

I take a baked offering outside at some point during the day when I'm observing Ewemeolc. It is always a loaf or cake that I have baked myself, because this imbues the gift with more meaning and value. Here in western Pennsylvania, the ground is often frozen solid and covered beneath a deep snow in late January and early February. This can make it awkward, if not entirely impossible, to plough or otherwise put the loaf into the earth as an offering to Hertha. When it would be unreasonable to try to bury the loaf, I simply set it on the ground and say a few words of thanks. Again, let me emphasize that you should find out if there are any local ordinances prohibiting you from setting out food.

Another option, if you live in the north and are organized enough to remember the necessary advance preparation, is to ready an offering site to Hertha in the late autumn before the ground freezes and snow begins to fall.

Dig a hole, removing the dirt to a shed or garage where you can keep it until Ewemeolc. Then insert an empty plastic jug or carton into the hole. This by itself looks sort of ugly, so you may want to cover it with a flat stone or patio brick. At Ewemeolc, remove the stone or brick, pull out the jug, and you have a hole in the ground that will serve as a functional offering site. Bury your cake offering in this hole using the dirt that you previously set aside.

During the Ewemeolc húsel itself, use milk as your offering. You are not likely to find ewe's milk in a supermarket today, but you may be able to find a bottle or small carton of goat's milk. Otherwise, offer a libation of whole cow's milk. For your opening prayer, as you raise your horn or cup, say something like,

> *Hertha, you who are called Mother of Men, we offer this milk in remembrance of your endless blessings. We give thanks for the ease in our lives, for the bounty we enjoy throughout the year, and we give thanks for the succor you gave to those who came before us. For our food, our clothes, our shelter—for all things we might otherwise take for granted—on this day we give thanks.*

In Nottinghamshire as late as the 1800s, people left candles burning in their homes on this day. This tradition may have no Pagan connection at all, but it certainly fits in with the spirit of the season. I like to leave a candle burning as a reminder of the increasing daylight hours that were so crucial to my ancestors' survival.

Eostre

In the English language, the Christian holiday of Easter takes its name from an Anglo-Saxon goddess of the spring, the dawn, and new beginnings. Eostre is only mentioned briefly by Bede, but the very fact that her name was preserved as the name of one of the most sacred days of Christendom is evidence of how important this goddess must have been to the early Anglo-Saxons. In other European languages what we know as Easter is called "Pasch," or some variant thereof.

Eostre also gives us our word for the direction of sunrise, the east. But she is not the sun itself, who, as we have seen, is an entity known to Saxon Pagans as the goddess Sunne.

Some Pagan people today celebrate Eostre's feast on the spring equinox, but it is more likely that her feast day was originally observed at the full moon following this. In the first place, the typical Anglo-Saxon farmer would have had a hard time knowing exactly when the equinox came. Equinox means "equal night," and comes twice a year, once in the spring and once in the autumn, when the days and nights are of equal length. In the spring this usually occurs on or near the twenty-first day of March. But calendars were not in widespread use in fifth century England, and almanacs were rarer still.

Furthermore, the Anglo-Saxons used a lunar calendar. Their month of April, known to them as Eostremonað, would have been determined by the moon's cycle. And we have the evidence of the later Christian tradition, which observes its Easter holiday on the first Sunday after the first full moon after the spring equinox. That is a rather odd way to commemorate what is presumably a historical date (the death and subsequent resurrection of Christ), but a very natural way to commemorate an earlier, lunar-based festival.

Whenever you decide to observe this holy tide, there is no question of who the honored deity will be at your húsel. During this mid-spring season, your offerings should always be directed to the goddess of spring and new beginnings, Eostre.

There is something exciting, almost sexy, about the feast of Eostre. The world is waking up around us and singing with delight. Even the animals seem to celebrate this holy tide, giving rise to expressions like "mad as a March hare." *Mad* in this case is not a reference to anger, but to the crazy, erratic behavior hares often exhibit during this exuberant season.

Eggs have been an Easter tradition for centuries. It probably dates back to the pre-Christian era, although to my knowledge there is no hard proof of this. It is often said that eggs are decorated at Easter to symbolize rebirth or new life. I tend to question this rather fanciful notion. Folklore is rarely quite so philosophical as this, and there is a much simpler explanation that better fits how pre-Christian Europeans related to the world around them.

We have already discussed how the spring holy tides celebrate the lengthening days. The effect of light on egg laying is staggering. In commercial egg production today, hens are exposed to long hours of artificial lighting to ensure maximum productivity. In an earlier, more natural time, productivity depended entirely on how many hours of sunlight there were in a day. During the Yuletide, poultry produced very few eggs. By Ewemeolc there was a noticeable increase in productivity. By Eostre, relatively speaking, the birds had turned into efficient little egg factories.

This would have been nearly as important to the early Anglo-Saxons as the lactation of their ewes. These eggs were a source of fresh food at a time when people were struggling for sustenance from one day to the next. What better offering for the goddess of spring, what better symbol of the bounty of the season, than the egg?

You can decorate your "Eostre eggs" in advance, but this can also be a fun activity for your inhíred to indulge in on the same day you hold your húsel. At one time eggs were decorated by boiling them with onion skins (for a golden color), spinach leaves (for green), and other natural dyes. Commercial dyes are easier to work with, but you may want to try these older techniques just for fun. If you are familiar at all with runes, you can use these symbols to decorate your eggs. Give Eostre's eggs time to dry thoroughly after you've colored them, and then use them to decorate your wéofod and as offerings to the goddess.

The Easter Bunny isn't actually English in origin, but instead comes from a German tradition of the Easter Hare that dates back at least as early as the sixteenth century. And there is absolutely no evidence of any connection between the hare or rabbit and the goddess Eostre. Nevertheless, this is one of those instances of "what would the

Saxons do now," where we see a very appropriate symbol of the season. Rabbits do not hibernate, but they do become less active in the winter to conserve their energy. In the spring they emerge again, excited and active, and so reflect the spirit of Eostre as she awakens the world each year.

May Day

The first of May is often associated with the Celtic holiday of Beltane and the "ancient Celtic tradition" of the Maypole. So it may come as some surprise that the Maypole is actually a Germanic custom unknown to Britain until the arrival of the Anglo-Saxons. Much later, in the sixteenth century, Philip Stubbes referred to the venerable pole as a "stinking idol." Beyond this, almost everything we know about the Maypole and the Pagan origins of its associated holiday is inference. Plaiting the pole with ribbons in a ritualized dance, which many people believe to be an old custom, is actually a nineteenth century innovation!

The old Saxon calendar is no help to us here. Bede tells us only that May was called Thrimilci because there were three milkings each day. The Anglo-Saxons loved their milk.

To better understand the meaning of May Day, we look to our Norse cousins, who celebrate Summerfinding and Winterfinding as two important turning points in the year. When we look at the many customs and superstitions associated with May Day, we can see that this is the English equivalent of Summerfinding. Summer began for the Anglo-Saxons at this time of year, not in the middle of June.

Today some Saxon Pagans celebrate May Day as a feast for the Wanic gods. One traditional English custom was to decorate horses with rosettes and flowers and have a horse procession. Horses are sacred to the god Ing. There may be no direct, obvious connection between Ing and these equine events, but for those who believe in the Wanic powers, who believe they are present still and continue to guide us, having an unbroken tradition going back a thousand years doesn't matter. What matters is that the old ways continue on. And this is what we find in most May Day traditions—customs at least superficially Christianized that nevertheless reflect the essential spirit of Summerfinding.

If the feast of Eostre has a sexy quality, May Day is positively lecherous. Opposition to May Day festivities in the sixteenth century and later focused primarily on what the celebrants were doing in the woods. And it wasn't bird watching.

One of the oldest May Day customs is that of "bringing in the May," gathering flowers and spring greenery and bringing them into the home. Or, to put it another way, going out and finding the new summer season. Depending on where you live, finding summer growth—especially flowering growth—may be difficult. England has a much milder climate than that found throughout much of North America. Nevertheless, depending on where you live, dandelions, forsythia, spirea, and other early blooming plants are often in flower by the first of May. Use these blossoms to decorate the wéofod, especially if you are celebrating the holiday indoors.

In an outdoor celebration, you could include a Maypole dance, complete with ribbons. This may be a new "tradition," but it fits in well with the ambience of May Day. You will need the pole itself, of course, which must be stable and at least eight to ten feet in height. You will also need one ribbon, about twice the length of this pole, for each of your dancers. The ribbons are tied at one end to the top of the pole.

As for the dancers, there must be an even number, and they need to be separated into two easily recognizable teams. Sometimes a group will divide by sex, males and females, but there are no rules for this. The only thing that matters is that your dancers can readily distinguish the "shirts" from the "skins." You could use two contrasting colors of ribbon, or have one team wear flowers in their hair, or you could literally divide your dancers up into shirts and skins!

These two teams take alternate positions around the pole, with each dancer holding the end of one ribbon. All of the "shirts" face one direction (i.e., clockwise) and all of the "skins" face the opposite direction (counterclockwise). One of these teams will be the first to go under the ribbons held by the other. Determine which team this is before the dance begins.

When the dance starts, the dancers alternate going over and under the ribbons held by the opposite team. And when we say "dance," we are using this word very loosely. Unless you have a professional dance team doing this, the dancers can skip, hop, or boogie however they wish. The important thing is that they remember to go over and under the ribbons in a continual pattern. As the dancers continue in circles around the pole, their ribbons will plait, or weave themselves down its length to form a colorful sheath.

If this seems too complicated but you still want a Maypole, forget about the ribbons. Just set up a pole somewhere and get your fellow hiredmenn to dance around it together. That is more traditional anyway.

Midsummer

This is the time of year American calendars so often insist on calling the "beginning" of summer. The summer solstice, falling on or near the twenty-first of June, is the longest day of the year. It was one of the most important holy tides in the Anglo-Saxon year, second only to Yule. The old name for this holiday is Litha ("LEE-tha"), a word probably related to the Old English *lith*, meaning "a point." The solstices are unique among our holy tides in that they are specific points in the solar year rather than lunar-based or seasonal celebrations.

The months we know as June and July were once called Ærra Litha and Æftera Litha, meaning, respectively, the moons or months before (*ærra*) and after (*æftera*) the turning point in the year when the days stop growing longer and begin to shorten. Of course today, with a calendar that only roughly corresponds with celestial movements, the solstice falls in the third week of June instead of at a point between two months.

Without a calendar to guide them, Anglo-Saxons would have had a difficult time knowing exactly when this Midsummer point occurred. This may be why it is a tradition not only in England but throughout all of Europe to celebrate the twenty-fourth of June as "Midsummer Day."

At Midsummer our lady Sunne, the sun, is in her full glory, and the traditions associated with Litha reflect this. The oldest and most enduring of these traditions is the bonfire, a fire below to honor the fire—the sun—above. If you cannot build an actual bonfire, some other flame, even if no larger than a candle, can be lit as a symbolic representation. In some rural areas, young people used to jump through the flames of the Midsummer bonfires. I am not going to say that doesn't still happen today, but I am also not going to recommend it, just because I don't want anyone holding me responsible if you fall into the fire.

Divinations, and in particular love divinations, are another Midsummer tradition. This is true to some degree for all of the holy tides, but Midsummer is often considered an especially magical season. Shakespeare made use of this in his *A Midsummer Night's Dream*, weaving a tale of fairies and impish illusions. The implication, from a Saxon perspective, is that the elves or nature spirits are more active and accessible at this time of year. And there is some logic to this. Although Sunne herself is not sovereign over the elves (a role filled by the god Ing), it makes sense that the denizens of the light-realm would be more available at the turning point when our own world is bathed in light. Obviously a húsel to Sunne is appropriate

at Midsummer, but be sure to leave offerings for your
Good Neighbors as well.

Lammas

This word comes from the Old English *hláfmæsse*, meaning "bread (or cake) festival." The suffix *mæsse* tells us
that this is a Christian name for the feast day, but the pre-
fix reveals its significance to the early Anglo-Saxons.
Lammas was the first of three harvest festivals. The official Christian date was set at August 1; however, Lammas
was essentially a celebration of the first wheat harvest.
Thus it is another seasonal holy tide. Originally it would
have taken place whenever the wheat was harvested,
which would vary depending on annual weather cycles.

Neo-Pagans often confuse Lammas with the Irish holiday of Lughnasadh. The latter is a funeral festival commemorating the death of Tailtiu, the mother of the Irish
god Lugh. Although the two festivals occur at roughly the
same time of year, they are not necessarily related. Lughnasadh was celebrated with contests of skill, sort of like
an Irish Olympics. Today, descriptions of Lughnasadh
often include some mention of "first fruits," but I think
this is another instance of somebody putting the ever-
popular Celtic label on an Anglo-Saxon tradition. A festival is not necessarily a "harvest celebration" just because
it takes place near or during a harvest season. The origin
of this expression—first fruits—is not Celtic. It was first
mentioned in an early ninth-century manuscript known
as the Anglo-Saxon Chronicle. In this document, it is the

feast of Lammas, not the Celtic Lughnasadh, that is described as "the feast of first fruits."

From this reference, we may infer that the holy tide was not limited to the celebration of the wheat harvest. "First fruits" is not a description we would expect for a feast focused exclusively on a grain harvest. Nevertheless, wheat was a significant crop in most Indo-European cultures. Bread making may have shaped European societies more than any other development throughout history. Lammas, with its ripening wheat, signaled the beginning of autumn and the coming harvest season.

Lammas is the bread festival, and bread is the theme. You can buy loaves at the supermarket, but there is no real substitute for freshly baked, homemade bread. The unmistakable aroma permeates the home as the dough rises, and even more so while the oven is giving it a hearty crust. Baking bread for a Lammas húsel is an activity that everyone can join in, or it might be the work of one especially talented híredmann. The loaf can be baked in the form of a man or animal, or braided, or shaped into a sort of wreath. Glaze the crust or leave it plain. If you are going to the trouble of baking your own bread, have fun with it. Lammas is, above all, a celebration. Make an ordinary wheat bread, or be more creative and knead in nuts or raisins or pieces of dried fruit.

Some inhírdas honor Thunor in their Lammas húsles, but there is no rule about this. I usually honor all of the gods, collectively, at this time of year.

The bread itself is your offering. Pass it around as you would pass the mead horn, letting each person pull off a small piece of bread. It is a good idea to also pass around a cup of mead or water directly after this, so the híredmenn have something to help them wash down the bread. The remainder of the loaf, of course, is then offered to whatever gods you are honoring at your Lammas húsel. If you are celebrating outside with a bonfire, the loaf can be placed in the flames. Otherwise it can be set either on the ground or on your wéofod, and buried later.

I like to divide the dough when we are baking our Lammas bread, reserving the largest portion for the group offering, and baking a number of smaller loaves to distribute among my fellow híredmenn and any guests who have joined us for our Lammas celebration. The participants can then take their loaves home and make personal offerings at their own household wéofodes or somewhere on their own land.

Harvest Home

Neo-Pagans today typically observe the mid-autumn harvest tide on the equinox, which comes on or near the twenty-first of September. But Harvest Home, obviously, celebrates the completion of the harvest, so it originally took place whenever the local crops had been brought in from the fields. This would vary considerably depending on the region, the crops in question, and the weather conditions in any given year. In the Christian era, as advancements led people away from a purely agrarian economy, the indigenous harvest festivals evolved into recurring traditions such as Michaelmas (September 29), where a roast goose was the central feature of the feast table. It was said that eating goose on Michaelmas Day would ensure prosperity throughout the following year.

Decorate your wéofod with symbols of the harvest: gourds, Indian corn, pumpkins. If you grow any vegetables or herbs of your own, these will provide a deeper, more personal appreciation of Harvest Home.

There are no universal Harvest Home traditions. In northern England, this holiday was often celebrated with a Mell Supper, a feast similar to the American tradition of Thanksgiving, but involving the entire village. The Mell Supper was often accompanied with a play or pageant. In one such play, a maiden sang with various male characters until finally deciding to "marry" one of them. In other villages, men in disguise would crash the supper, with the other participants at least pretending to resist the intrusion.

A Saxon inhíred can hold its own Mell Supper by making its húsel the focal point of a harvest feast. The Harvest Home table should present a sense of abundance, much as the American Thanksgiving table does. The main dish can be either a traditional goose or a turkey, or, for a smaller group, even a roast chicken. If your híredmenn are all vegetarians, the bird can be dispensed with entirely. If you have a vegetable garden, try to include at least a token of your own harvest somewhere in the dinner. A libation of mead is appropriate for an offering if you have nothing else. The ideal offering would be something you harvested yourself, which could even be the aforementioned mead libation if you harvest your own honey! Whatever you choose, be sure to set out an offering bowl on your feast table if it is any distance from the household wéofod. The god Ing is often honored during this holy tide, but this is a matter of personal choice.

Another recurring traditional harvest theme is an effigy known variously as the Harvest Queen, Corn Queen, or Corn Baby. This image, made from dried leaves and stalks, is usually human shaped and may be richly dressed. The Corn Queen was sometimes hung in the barn or home until the following year. Corn in this instance, of course, doesn't mean maize, although maize is indeed a type of corn. The Old English word *corn* meant any seed, grain, or berry. Hence our word *acorn*, meaning the seed of the oak (Old English: *ác-corn*). The largest seasonal harvest in any region was typically a grain harvest, but a truly traditional Corn Queen or Corn Baby should be constructed of material related to your own local harvest, whether or not this is a grain. I have seen a doll such as this crafted of dried wormwood by a woman who grows and sells herbs for a living. For preserving the spirit of the tradition, this is certainly more valid than her creating a Corn Queen from plants unrelated to her livelihood.

The Corn Queen can be kept on the wéofod, or over the hearth, or perhaps hung somewhere in the kitchen. The following spring, perhaps during the feast of Eostre, set the image either in your garden or in some wild place as a special offering to the elves.

Hallows

Just as May Day marks the beginning of summer, the holy tide that comes at the end of October—observed as the secular celebration of Halloween—is the Saxon Winterfinding.

This is seen in the Anglo-Saxons' name for the month of October, which they called *Winterfylleth*, or "winter-tide." The Norse celebrated Winterfinding earlier in the season, but in Germany it merged with the Christian holiday of Martinmas (November 11) and in England with All Hallows. The Celts also had a holiday near the end of October, Samhain, and some attribute the date of the Anglo-Saxon celebration to Celtic influence, but it may have had more to do with England's milder climate. One does not celebrate the beginning of winter when winter is still six weeks away.

Whatever the reason for the shift in date, Hallows was the beginning of the Blótmonað, the month of blood sacrifice. This was the third and final harvest of the year, the harvest of livestock. All of the animals that could not be fed over the winter were butchered. This was a time of feasting, and much of the slaughtering was ritualized (the blood sacrifice) to give thanks to the gods. Meat that could not be consumed was salted down or hung in chimneys to dry.

The beginning of winter is also the start of the "wild hunt" when Woden is said to ride through the countryside with a pack of hounds, gathering up the lost souls of the dead. The hunt continues into November and December, and throughout the Yuletide.

Saxon Pagans today will often hold húsles for their ancestral spirits at Hallows. There is no evidence that the early Anglo-Saxons did anything like this, but there is also no evidence that they did not, and the custom is fitting for this season. Winter has come, and the world is dying, or at least settling down for a very long nap. This is a liminal time between the seasons. Many Pagans feel a close connection with the spirits of the dead during the holy tide of Hallows.

One popular and deeply meaningful custom is that of the dumb supper. So far as I can tell, the dumb supper as a tradition has its origins not in Anglo-Saxon England or Celtic Ireland, but in the backwoods of rural America. And I may be slightly biased toward this tradition, because it is most often documented in the region of the Ozark Mountains where I spent part of my childhood. The traditional dumb supper originally was most often a magical act of divination for young women to learn who their future husbands would be.

Nevertheless, the dumb supper has always had close associations with the dead (who would reveal the information about the future husbands), and a modified version is frequently enacted now as a Hallows húsel. It is called a "dumb" supper because nobody speaks throughout the meal. Instead, participants think about their ancestors and deceased loved ones as they eat, and listen for any words or feelings that those spirits might impart to the living.

Sometimes one person will prepare the entire meal, but one custom I have come to especially appreciate is for all of the participants to contribute dishes that remind them of their ancestors for one reason or another. This works best if one of your híredmenn coordinates what everyone brings, just to make sure your dinner doesn't consist entirely of nine varieties of cookies. Trust me, this can happen very easily if you do not have an advance plan. One solution is for the host to provide a main dish—something connecting him to his ancestors—and for the other híred-menn to bring side dishes. When people arrive for the húsel, everyone is allowed to speak normally until the meal formally begins. The various dishes should be laid out on a table, and one empty plate set in a place of honor for the ancestors.

When the dinner is to begin, the ealdor, or whoever is leading the rite, places a helping of his own contribution on the ancestors' plate, explaining why he chose that particular dish and how it connects him to his ancestors. Then all of the híredmenn do the same, adding another food to the plate and sharing some memory of their own ancestors.

Assuming that the dumb supper is held indoors, the ealdor then opens a door to the home and invites in the ancestors, saying,

Ancestors! You who have gone before, you who have brought each of us to where we are today, we welcome you to our feast. A plate has been set for you, our honored guests. Join us, and share with us, and know that you are remembered, now and always.

This is also the signal for everyone to stop talking. From now until the ealdor formally ends the supper, nobody is to speak a single word. It should go without saying that this rite is unsuitable for any children who may be too young to remain silent throughout the meal. However, I have seen children as young as seven or eight participate in dumb suppers and appreciate the richness of the experience as much as any adult. At one supper, a very young girl came forward to put some candy on the ancestral plate for her pet rabbit that had recently died. There was not a dry eye in the room as she solemnly turned and took her own place at the table.

People report different experiences during a dumb supper. For some it is nothing more or less than a quiet time to reflect on one's ancestors. But other people occasionally experience visions, sounds, odors, or feelings that have no mundane explanation.

When everyone has finished eating, the ealdor ends the supper by thanking the ancestors. They are not dismissed. These are guests, not summoned servants. Although the supper is done, the ancestors themselves are welcomed to stay as long as they will. Thanking the ancestors is also a signal that people may again speak aloud.

Yule

The annual cycle comes full circle with the Yuletide, the grandest celebration of the year. People often confuse this with the winter solstice (December 21), but Yule is a season, not a particular day. The solstice, known to the Anglo-Saxons as Módraniht, is the first night of a celebration of feasting, family, and fellowship lasting twelve days or longer.

Most inhírdas will hold a húsel on Módraniht to honor their idesa, or female ancestors, as described in the sixth chapter. But the celebrations that follow in the wake of this húsel vary greatly from one group to another.

If you have a fondness for the Christian traditions related to Christmas, you'll be pleased to know that many of these are equally suitable for a Saxon celebration of the Yuletide. Don't read more into this than what I have said. No matter what you may hear from others, very few Christmas customs are ancient Pagan traditions. But that does not concern the modern Saxon Pagan. These same customs, whatever their origins, were very often devised by descendants of the Anglo-Saxons and still reflect the worldview inherent in that culture.

Consider the example of the Yule tree, which we discussed at the beginning of this chapter. An ancient tradition less than three hundred years old really is not all that ancient. And yet the Yule tree can be a beautiful representation of Anglo-Saxon cosmology, a symbol of the great tree that connects the Seven Worlds. This World Tree was sometimes described, historically, as a large evergreen tree, the European yew. In the Christian era, yew trees were planted in churchyards throughout England. Before this, an enormous evergreen yew was a prominent feature at the Temple of Uppsala, in Sweden, where the old gods were once honored.

In my household, we decorate the Yule tree with the images of birds and animals, artificial apples, and colored glass balls. There is nothing overtly "Pagan" in its appearance. A stranger walking into our living room during the Yuletide would never guess, from the tree standing there, that we were a Pagan family. (The wéofod next to the tree, of course, is a dead giveaway.) Our tree looks pretty much like the trees that our Christian neighbors put up in their homes. And this is important to me, as a Saxon Pagan, because another function of the Yule tree is to connect me to my ancestors, who for the past fifteen hundred years have mostly been Christians. An eighteenth-century tradition may not be very old, but it is a tradition that my own grandparents observed, and their grandparents before them.

The only Yuletide custom of real antiquity is the wassail bowl. *Wassail* is an Old English greeting (*wes hal*) meaning "be whole" or "be healthy." Once, long ago, there were two distinct traditions of wassailing. The first tradition involved going out to the local orchards, singing to the trees, and making offerings of hard cider. The second tradition was usually practiced by young women, who would carry a bowl of spiced ale or hard cider from door to door, singing to their neighbors much as carolers do today. Today the Saxon Pagan can capture the spirit of these traditions by setting out a wassail bowl at any Yuletide gathering.

There are literally hundreds of wassail recipes, varying from simple to daunting. The only ground rule is that the drink consist largely of either ale or cider. Hard cider is traditional, but many people today use sweet apple cider.

The following recipe is really easy and makes a delicious wassail you can serve at your Yule húsel. It is non-alcoholic, so children as well as adults can enjoy it during this holy tide. You will need a large pot, a gallon of apple cider, a tea ball, seven cloves, seven whole allspice, and seven cinnamon sticks. Pour the apple cider into the pot, and put this on your stove to simmer. Place the cloves and allspice into the tea ball, and drop this into the cider. Add the cinnamon sticks. These can float in the cider as it simmers for the next thirty to forty-five minutes.

If you are feeling really ambitious, slice up an orange and a lemon, and throw the pieces in. But that part is optional.

In my household, we observe Yule for twelve days. The Twelve Days of Christmas is not especially Pagan in origin. It is an old Christian tradition established by the Council of Tours in 567 CE. The duration of the Yule season probably varied regionally in pre-Christian Anglo-Saxon society, although it almost certainly began everywhere on Módraniht. Some Pagans today continue celebrating Yule as late as mid-January, but a twelve-day observance brings the Yuletide to an end just after New Year's, and that feels right to me. As a personal "tradition," I always leave a special offering to the elves on the last day of Yule, on or near the second of January.

Just as there is no set duration for the Yuletide, there are no standard traditions for celebrating these days. Inhírdas usually evolve their own traditions, and this is perhaps more "traditional" than any contrived, standardized list. If you live in a rural area, you could revive the old practice of wassailing orchard trees, but Saxon Pagans living in downtown Kansas City probably are not going to be doing anything like that. Instead they might get together, fill a wassail bowl, and spend the evening singing songs around a piano.

When deciding what customs to incorporate into your Yuletide, keep in mind the real reason for the season. There are very few hours of daylight at this time of year. For the early Anglo-Saxons, this meant that there wasn't much to do. Even indoors, trying to accomplish any detailed work with the flickering of firelight is difficult at best. Like Midsummer, the midwinter holy tide recognized a specific turning point in the year, this time on Módraniht, after which the hours of daylight would begin to increase. And because the nights were so long, this was an ideal time to settle in with friends, family, and neighbors, to reflect on the past year and make plans for the coming year. The theme for the Yuletide, therefore, is family and community.

The Yule candle is a nineteenth-century tradition that fits in very well with the spirit of this season. It is most likely an adaptation of the Yule log. These tall candles were lit on Christmas Eve and burned throughout the night and following day. As a further adaptation for a specifically Saxon Pagan observance, a large Yule candle can be lit on each of the twelve nights. Allow the candle to burn for a set duration, perhaps an hour each night. Or arrange twelve smaller candles on your household wéofod, lighting one the first night, two the second, and so forth, until all twelve are burning on the last night of Yule.

———

These holy tides can feel especially lonely for the solitary Saxon Pagan, but they need not be. These are times when friends and family members can be included even if they don't follow your path. In America today, almost everyone decorates a Yule tree and dyes Eostre eggs, even if they call them by other names. These activities have become secular and disassociated from Christian religious symbolism, if indeed there ever was any. (I have never quite understood what a pine tree has to do with the birth of Christ.) And as we have seen, they are entirely appropriate activities for the Saxon holy tides.

Friends or family members who are open minded may even be willing to join you in baking bread for Lammas, or holding a Mell Supper at the equinox. Do not be offended if they politely refuse, but instead be pleasantly surprised if they think enough of you to help you celebrate the season. The Saxon Pagan never tries to convert friends, or to force them into doing anything they're uncomfortable with. But there is also nothing in our traditions that demands or encourages you to become a misanthropic hermit. When and if you can share the joy of our holy tides with your loved ones, whether or not they follow the path of the Saxon Pagan, by all means do so.

Rites of Passage

We have seen how Saxon inhírdas gather for monthly húsles and for the seasonal holy tides. Another reason for an inhíred to get together is a rite of passage. It is at a time like this when community becomes especially important.

A rite of passage is any ritualized moment in which a person's status or definition changes in a perceptible way. The gesithscipe oath described in the ninth chapter is an example of a rite of passage. Before giving the oath, the individual has no binding obligation to his fellow híredmenn, nor they to him. He is more like a friend of the family rather than an integral member. The oath changes this status. In giving his oath, he becomes a gesith, a full peer of his fellows.

Most of these life passages are events that all of us go through—birth, puberty, marriage, death. Sometimes the rite is confused with the event. A rite of passage is a community acknowledgment of something that has already occurred. A wedding does not create a marriage. It acknowledges a condition that already exists. Today this condition is the bond of affection between two people. When marriages were arranged, the condition was a political or social agreement between two tribes or families, a pact often sealed years earlier.

Similarly, the words spoken by the new gesith are an acknowledgment of something that has already taken place in that person's heart. The ealdor's reply acknowledges a decision that the inhíred has already arrived at collectively. The gesithscipe oath, like every rite of passage, is a community's way of certifying or recognizing a change in a person's status that has already taken place.

Naming

The first passage each of us goes through occurs when we first emerge into this Middle Earth. The nine parts of the soul are bound to the body when we take our first breath. It is at this point that our status changes to what might be called "personhood."

The rite acknowledging this is the Namian, or the Naming ceremony. To give something a name is to empower it. During the Namian, the parents acknowledge their child and present him or her to the community. This is a joyous occasion, when the parents' fellow gesithas welcome the young *hiredcniht* ("HEAR-ed-k-night") into their extended family.

The Naming ceremony is only held after the child has settled into the home and is stable and healthy. Newborn infants are delicate, and the well-being of the child is always the first consideration. A second consideration is the well-being of the parents. People who have to get up every two hours throughout the night to feed and change a newborn infant are unlikely to be in any mood for a ritual the next day. If the parents so choose, the Naming can certainly be held when the child is only a week or two old, but six months or even older is not uncommon.

This rite can be held during the celebration of a holy tide if the parents desire. Some parents like to do this, while others prefer the Naming to be a special occasion focused entirely on their child. If the Naming is held in conjunction with a húsel, as is most often the case, the former should take place after offerings have been made to the honored deity. This ensures that the deity is present to witness the Naming.

Fire is carried around the ritual area as usual. After this comes the seasonal or monthly húsel, if one is being given. Before the closing prayer (or after the ritual space has been claimed, if there is no húsel) the ealdor turns to the parents and asks,

Did you have some purpose to bring before us?

The parents should bring the child to the wéofod, and face their fellow híredmenn. Either parent can speak for the child here. The parent will say,

We bring our child before you, a son of [name of in-híred]. *Look upon him and know him.*

(I'm using the masculine gender here. You would of course use appropriate wording for a daughter.)

The ealdor should echo this, saying to all híredmenn present,

Look upon this child.

Taking the child around for each of the gesithas to see, the parent repeats,

Look upon him and know him.

The ealdor now asks,

How shall we know him? By what name would you call him?

Addressing the child, the parent says,

I name you [child's name], *son of* [parent's name], *son of* [grandparent's name].

This lineage can be given however the parents desire, and both may take part in it if they wish. The child is being identified here, and his ancestral heritage acknowledged. There is no reason why all of the grandparents cannot be acknowledged, or why more distant generations cannot be mentioned while giving the child's lineage.

The ealdor then says,

Folk of [name of inhíred], *look upon* [name of child], *son of* [mother's name] *and* [father's name], *and know that he is one of our own. May Frige watch over our child; may Thunor protect him and Woden inspire him. Wes* [name of child] *hal!*

All present repeat,

Wes [name of child] *hal!*

This is an example of a Saxon Namian. My example should not be viewed as the "official Naming ceremony," because there is no such thing. You see here the important steps. The parents present their child for their fellow gesithas to view. They formally name the child, and the ealdor acknowledges this and invokes the blessings of the gods. But the parents can and very often will include other elements in this basic pattern.

Parents will sometimes name another adult—perhaps, but not necessarily, one of their fellow híredmenn—as a godfather or godmother of the child. The godparent is asked to watch over the child and ensure his spiritual growth. Oaths between the parents and the godparent may be exchanged. Over the years, a close bond can form between the godparent and godchild, and the parents know that their child has another adult to turn to for counsel.

In some Naming ceremonies, the híredmenn, or at least the gesithas, will come forward with gifts for the child. This can be something like a postpartum baby shower; however, the gifts may also be items that the child will not use for many years to come. The parents might be given a fine knife, for example, to pass on when the child comes of age.

And what if the parents do not belong to an inhíred? If both parents are Saxon Pagans, this is a contradiction. Two parents, and now a child, equal a household. Even if the household doesn't extend beyond these three, it is nevertheless an inhíred. The parents may wish to invite friends to witness the Namian. There is no ealdor to speak, so those lines are omitted. The parents themselves lead the rite, naming and presenting their child to their gods, and to any witnesses attending. When the Namian is a private rite involving only the parents and the child, the wording will of course be much less formal. The child is named, along with his lineage, and one parent invokes the blessings of the gods.

Adulthood

One rite of passage found in most early societies that we have lost today is a ritual marking the transition into adulthood. As we mature, we gain certain rights—such as the right to drink, or the right to vote—but for most people there is no moment of formal recognition as a peer by the adult community.

Long ago, young men throughout northern Europe proved their worth by hunting a wild species of cattle known as the aurochs. These great beasts had disappeared from Britain by the 1200s, and were extinct throughout Europe by the early part of the seventeenth century. Obviously nobody is going to be hunting aurochs today. Nor is hunting any creature a necessary element of a rite of passage into adulthood. The youths who hunted the aurochs were proving their worth as men in a society in which hunting was an integral part of the economy. The horns of the aurochs would be shaped into mead horns, its hide into leather goods, its meat used for sustenance.

That was then. This is now.

Hunting can be and sometimes is a rite of passage, especially in rural communities. But for many people today, this would be a meaningless act with no connection to adulthood. Remember, the defining quality of a rite of passage is the community's acknowledgment of the change in a person's status.

When we talk about the change to adulthood, many people immediately think of puberty rites. But here again we need to consider the world we live in today. Puberty and "adulthood" are no longer the same thing. Our society is more complicated now.

If puberty itself is not our measure, how are we to know when a person is ready to be acknowledged as an adult? I don't think there is any single answer to this. In general, it is when that person is ready and willing to join in the adults' activities. He must be willing to take on responsibility—the work, as well as the fun—and be accountable for his own actions. He must, in the eyes of his community, be prepared to conduct himself as a peer.

In this way, the gesithscipe oath becomes the rite of passage into adulthood within the inhíred. If the household is one of choice, most híredmenn will probably give this oath as adults. But the function of the gesithscipe oath is to establish peerage, so the same oath is used when a híredcniht, or child, is ready to declare himself an equal adult member of the household. A híredcniht should be physically "adult," that is, well into puberty. And presumably this oath would only be accepted from a young person who has also demonstrated mental and emotional maturity.

The young adult gives the oath exactly as any other híredmann would. The only exception is that he addresses the oath to his father and mother, even if the ealdor of the inhíred should be somebody other than his parents.

It is possible that the child, as he matures to adulthood, may be called to follow some other religion. It is only natural for any parent to want his offspring to follow his own path, but as a polytheist, the Saxon Pagan recognizes that each person must be free to follow his heart. There are gods other than our own, and customs different from but as valid as our own. If a young person chooses to honor the Hellenic gods, or the Roman or Egyptian gods, this is his right. And if he does choose to follow a foreign path, the gesithscipe oath is no longer appropriate for him. He may, of course, remain a híredmann, or family member, but his own path must be respected.

Marriage

The child is born, grows, and eventually matures into adulthood. And then a day comes, for many, when affection leads to another of life's passages.

Marriage is a union on all levels, physical as well as spiritual, between two consenting adults. There are people today who would define in a very narrow way what a "traditional" marriage is, even though there is nothing truly traditional about any modern marriage.

Let us look at what a truly traditional marriage would be like. "Traditionally" you would not even have a say as to who your spouse would be. You would marry whoever your father said you were going to marry. The choice might have little, if anything, to do with your own interests. Your spouse would most likely be chosen because your dad wanted something from your betrothed's dad, or vice versa. If you are the bride, after the wedding, before you and your husband departed for your honeymoon, your lord—whomever your husband has sworn fealty to—would have the option of being the first to have sex with you. You would not have a say in this either. We do not live in any kind of feudal system today, so the lord in question would probably be your husband's employer or manager.

That is your traditional marriage. Take it or leave it.

Throughout most of history, marriage has been primarily a political institution having only a coincidental association with love or affection. However, our concepts of both marriage and family have evolved. Families today come in many forms, and marriage in the twenty-first century can likewise manifest in different ways. As a rite of passage, we are viewing marriage as a change in a person's—in this case, two persons'—status. Two people are joining together in a complete union. That is, a union that is ideally both physical and spiritual. Their orlay is woven together forever. Yes, forever. Even if the marriage should fail, neither spouse will be exactly the same as before.

Because it is such an important, irreversible step, each partner should have good, sound reasons for undertaking this rite of passage. Love, by itself, is not enough. Love is an emotion, a feeling. And while it may be a very pleasant feeling, love can evaporate as quickly as it arrived when there is no reason nor argument to support it. You should know, in no vague or uncertain terms, why you want to marry this person.

If the secular government will recognize your marriage, it is usually a good idea to go through the necessary legal proceedings for this. Legal recognition of the marriage will give you countless perks and protections that other couples do not enjoy. The marriage contract itself, however, is between the couple and their gods. If two people are making a commitment to one another, then they are the ones who should define the terms of agreement. The clearer those terms are, the greater the likelihood that the marriage will last. Neither person should assume that the other intuitively knows what is expected of him or her. Do both partners want children, and, if so, how many? What about pets? And when it comes to the opposite (or same) sex, what behavior is acceptable, and what is not?

Who will be the primary breadwinner? If both partners intend to pursue their careers equally, what are the limitations? It is important to discuss issues like this before one spouse learns that his or her company is relocating its offices to another city.

Religion itself should be among the terms of agreement. Personally, I would not consider marriage to a non-Pagan. To marry somebody who I am not connected to spiritually, for me, is no different than marrying somebody who I am not going to connect with physically. But there are a lot of spiritually mixed marriages that work just fine. For that matter, there are marriages in which the spouses are virtually celibate, and those seem to work too. A marriage can be defined by almost any set of parameters. The important thing is that both parties have a clear understanding of what they are buying into. If your spouse-to-be is not a polytheist, does he or she understand exactly what this entails? Will there be any objection to you honoring your gods with offerings? To you sharing your beliefs and practices with your children?

The marriage itself is a complex oath, as binding as any other. Understand fully what you are promising. I do not believe in making an "until death do we part" oath. Again, this is a personal call, but I value my marriage too much to place such a heavy burden on it. "Until death" is literally a life sentence, and it can feel very much that way during those rocky times that every marriage must endure. My own marriage oath has always been for a limited duration, usually seven years, with an option to renew. It is much more feasible, more honest I think, to say, "I promise that I will stick by you, no matter what, and do my best to make this marriage work for the next seven years." Or three years, or five years. This is a promise you can reasonably keep.

If you are already married and have sworn "until death," know that I am not criticizing what you have done in any way. On the contrary, I think it is great that you have managed to give an oath like this and make it work. But the seven-year plan has worked very well for me, so I'm sticking with that.

Once you have decided that you do, indeed, want to marry, and you and your partner have worked out the seemingly endless details of this agreement, there are almost as many decisions to make about the rite itself. You can, of course, just take a rite such as the one I give below and use that, but most Pagan couples today like to design their own weddings. What follows should be considered an example only.

The rite is facilitated either by a Saxon druid or by a wéofodthegn. I am going to say "druid" here for the sake of simplicity. Also for simplicity, I am going to say "bride and groom." If this is a same-sex wedding, alter the wording accordingly.

On the wéofod there should be two unlit candles, a horn filled with mead, the two rings that the couple will exchange, an offering bowl, and a wéoh (image or representation) of the goddess Frige.

The druid or an assistant begins the rite by carrying fire in the form of a lantern or candle and walking around the ritual area in order to claim it. As with any rite, say,

I carry fire around this holy stead, and ask all spirits to depart unless invited in. Thunor, ward this sacred place. Let this be a day of joy and celebration.

Addressing all those present, the druid says,

We gather today to witness and bless the wedding of [bride] and [groom], and to support their union by our community of faith and family. May the gods, the ancestors, and the spirits of this land bless this rite.

The bride and groom now come forward and stand before the wéofod, the Saxon altar. The druid turns to them and says,

> [Bride] *and* [groom], *you are about to embark on a new journey. As your paths converge, let each of you remember how you have come to this place, and give thanks to those who have brought you here.*

The bride now lights one of the two candles on the wéofod. She addresses her ancestors, giving thanks and asking for their blessing. This is extremely personal, so the words should be her own. It is not inappropriate for the bride to name significant ancestors who she wants to honor at this time. The simplest, most minimal wording might go something like this:

> *Ancestors—mothers of my mothers—I give thanks to you this day, and ask for your blessing. Know that you will be remembered and honored always by me and my husband.*

The groom then lights his ancestral candle. While his wording should also be personal, it should complement what the bride has said. The couple should have worked this out in advance, so that one is not rambling on for twenty minutes, thanking every great-grandparent and distant aunt by name, while the other has nothing similar prepared. After all, you do not want the ancestors on one side of the family to feel slighted. If the bride gave the above minimal wording, the groom could follow with this:

Ancestors—fathers of my fathers—I give thanks to you this day, and ask for your blessing. Know that you will be remembered and honored always by me and my wife.

The druid, turning to the wéofod, now says,

Frige, we ask that you bless this couple and their marriage. May they each be a blessing to the other, and to their united kin. May their luck grow ever stronger. May Tiw bind and strengthen the agreements between them. May Thunor protect them, and may Woden inspire their years ahead.

To the bride and groom, the druid says,

As the gods have joined us in this place to witness this union, so should you now make oaths, one to the other, in their presence.

The groom now places a ring on the bride's finger, giving her his personal oath and ending with the words, "With this ring, I wed thee." The bride then does the same. This is without question the most intimate part of the ceremony. As an example of a very simple oath, each partner might say,

In the years ahead, I will guard and protect you, love and nurture you, inspire and encourage you. I will stand by you in good times and bad, to the best of my ability. With this ring, I wed thee.

But this is an example only. If you cannot think of anything more to say to somebody whom you may be spending the rest of your life with, maybe you should reconsider the whole marriage idea.

After the rings have been exchanged, the druid invites the couple to kiss, takes up the horn of mead, and says,

In the tradition of our people, oaths are sworn over the mead of inspiration. Let us honor this day the union of [bride] *and* [groom].

The druid takes a sip from the horn and passes it to the groom, who toasts the bride. The horn then goes to the bride, who toasts the groom. After this the bride and groom should take the horn around to their wedding guests, allowing each to toast the marriage in turn. At a large wedding the mead horn may need to be refilled several times.

After the horn has been passed to all of the guests, it is returned to the druid, who pours the remaining mead into the offering bowl, saying, "To the gods!" At this time the bride and groom may also want to give an additional offering of some kind, as a couple, to the goddess Frige.

The druid now turns the new couple to face their guests and says, "I present to you [bride] and [groom]." This signals the end of the marriage rite.

The Final Journey

Eventually we all will come to the passage that few people want to think about, much less talk about. Our own mortality is impossible to fully comprehend. It is unknowable, and that makes it frightening. We try not to look at death, and when facing it becomes unavoidable, all of the platitudes and truisms in the world are little more than bandages on the gaping wounds of our grief.

The traditions and beliefs held by Saxon Pagans focus on how we live, and in this way we also understand something of death. We will become ancestors in some way—ancestors of the heart, or of the land, if not ancestors of blood. But what happens beyond this depends on our deeds during our lives. There is no one answer, nor is it a simple either/or division like the Christians' heaven and hell.

The Saxon Pagan sees the human being as not just a body and soul, but consisting of many parts. One of these parts is the body (Old English: *líc*), but there are nine other parts that might be considered the "soul," all bound together and to the body by the æthem, or life force. Thus it is possible that after death we might find ourselves not in one final resting place, but several.

For the moment, however, let us focus on the part of a person known as the *mód* (pronounced like "mode"). This is the person's sense of identity, and is perhaps the closest thing to the idea of a soul. Where does this one facet of the self depart after the æthem fades away and releases it? For most of us, the mód will journey to the realm of Hel, a dark but otherwise neutral world. What we find there will depend on what we did when we were alive. Hopefully, we will be welcomed joyfully into the halls of our ancestors.

Many Saxon Pagans believe that those who journey to Hel will rest there for a time, and then return to Middle

Earth. Some say these módes are reborn into their own bloodlines, returning as their own descendants. Is this so? There is no way of knowing for certain, and so there is no point in debating or worrying about it. I believe some are reborn when they have a need to return to Middle Earth, whereas others remain in the realm of the dead, perhaps forever. But don't ask me to prove this.

The lore of the northern European people teaches us that some never make the journey to Hel at all. Of those who die in battle, half are chosen by Woden and half by Fréo. These are taken to the celestial halls in Osgeard that are maintained by the two deities. Does this include everyone who dies in combat? Maybe. Again, there is no way to know. But if Woden and Fréo claim even some of our módes, we can be reasonably certain that the other gods and goddesses do the same. However, those who are chosen are not necessarily being rewarded. It might be more accurate to say they are being called into service.

Consider those who are carried up to Walhall, or what the Norse call Valhalla. In Norse myth, these valiant warriors feast all day, and then fight until they are killed. The next day they start all over again. This is not my idea of a good time. The thought of facing a gory and painful death each day is not very appealing to me, but I am sure anyone going through that will develop a great fighting technique. And that, I believe, is the truth behind this myth. I don't know that the glorious warriors of Walhall literally die every twenty-four hours, but I am pretty sure Woden has some purpose in mind—an undoubtedly challenging purpose—for any soul he collects for himself. In Scandinavian myth, he is said to be building an army in preparation for Ragnarok, a hypothetical battle in the future when the gods will go to war against the giants. I personally believe that the idea of Ragnarok was inspired by the Christian vision of Armageddon. There is no mention of this catastrophic event in Old English literature.

I would like to think that my lord Ing might take me up with the elves in their realm of light when the time comes that I must leave Middle Earth. But the more realistic part of me suspects that I will be going to Hel. And that is all right too, I suppose. I have family there, and friends.

Death is the most difficult and incomprehensible of life's passages, not only for the person dying, but also for those left behind. This is especially true for those who have lost a spouse or a child, because in these relationships a part of our own identity is also lost forever. But whatever relationship a survivor had with the deceased, it's important to remember that the resulting grief is intensely private. You don't "know exactly how they feel," so don't say something like that. Honor the fact that the survivor is feeling something you can't possibly know, even if you've been through a similar experience.

Death often brings out the most irrational emotions within us. We may even resent the person who died, feeling a sense of abandonment. This is a time when people may lash out at each other. People hurt, and when people hurt they can be mean. If the deceased's blood kin are not Pagan, it is very possible that they will bury that person with rites and customs diametrically opposed to what he or she would have wished. And they will almost always have the legal (if not ethical) right to do so.

This means that the chosen family of a Saxon Pagan, the other gesithas and híredmenn, may be left with no personal remains to honor after that individual's death if they are not also related to the deceased by blood. The solution to this is to give some personal remains to the inhíred before one's death. Hair is a dead part of the body that we discard periodically throughout our lives. Although the hair cells are quite dead, they still contain our DNA. They are still a part of us. (This is why hair is often used as a "link" in magic spells.) Hair can be collected and given to the ealdor or to a trusted loved one for safekeeping.

The hair can then be honored as the body would have been if that person's blood kin had respected his or her path. It can be buried respectfully and allowed to return to the earth, burned ritually, or even kept in a jar or urn of some kind.

Whatever approach you take, this final rite of passage should always serve the needs of those who were closest to the deceased while simultaneously respecting the wishes and beliefs of the deceased. If the deceased had a particularly close relationship with a god or goddess, a húsel might be held for that deity. The rite of passage itself, however, usually takes the form of a memorial. The inhíred gathers with any friends or loved ones sympathetic to the deceased's Saxon beliefs. To maintain some order to the proceedings, an item of some kind is passed around. This may be the deceased's remains (hair) or some object that held a special meaning for him or her. Only the person holding that object is allowed to speak.

The object is passed among the participants, giving each person the opportunity to describe a favorite memory of the deceased. For some people it may be too difficult to speak, and it is perfectly acceptable to hold the object for a moment and then pass it on. If the deceased had a favorite poem, this might be read aloud by one of the participants. Often a photograph will be set out. Since the deceased is now officially an ancestral spirit, offerings may be given. Whether or not there is a photograph, whether there are offerings to the deceased, all depends on the needs and wishes of those left behind, presuming these respect the wishes of the deceased. It may be too soon for ancestral offerings. Emotions are raw at this time.

At the end of the memorial there should be some act of closure. This can be the burial or burning of the remains, but it can take any form that allows the participants to bid farewell to their loved one. At one memorial I attended, the participants wrote short farewell notes to the deceased. These were tied to strings attached to helium balloons, and at the end of the rite everyone released their balloons at the same time. The balloons ascended together into the sky, in a circular formation, bearing our good wishes to another realm, and lifting our hearts to worlds beyond this Middle Earth.

———

King Penda, when he looks down from Walhall in Osgeard, must surely be pleased to see that there are still

Pagan Saxons all over the globe making due offerings to the gods of their ancestors, teaching their children of honor, of loving and living, growing and giving. Nearly fifteen centuries have passed since Penda was killed on the banks of the Winwaed. But, as they say, it isn't over until the fat lady sings. Let us pray—to Woden and Frige and Thunor—that we never hear that sad lament.

Glossary

Ælf ("alf"): A discarnate or disembodied spirit. An elf. This includes any pure spiritual being, including dwarves and ancestral spirits. In a more specific sense, "elf" refers to a nature spirit, or land wight.

Æthem ("A-them"): The life force, binding all parts of the "self" together. The breath of life.

Boggart ("BOGG-art"): A frightening spirit. The term comes from northern England, and may be derived from the Welsh *bwg*, meaning a ghost.

Brosingamen ("BROE-sing-gam-en"): Fréo's golden necklace Brosingamen was crafted by four dwarves. The necklace is referred to in *Beowulf*, lines 1197–2000.

Drýcræft ("DRU-craft"): The skill or art of the Saxon druid. Magical skill.

Drýmann ("DRU-man"): A Saxon druid. Related to the Gaelic *draoi*, meaning a druid or wizard.

Dwarfhame ("DWARF-fame"): The realm or world directly beneath Middle Earth. The dark womb or caverns where "potential" is forged into material manifestation.

Ealdor ("EH-al-dor"): The Old English word for "elder" or "head of the family." Often used as a functional description for the leader of an inhíred.

Elfhame ("ELF-fame"): The realm or world directly above Middle Earth. This is the domain of the light elves, who help nurture the woodlands and other natural places in our own physical dimension.

Eormensyl ("EH-or-men-sul"): The World Tree. The Eormensyl is the *axis mundi* that connects all planes of existence.

Eostre ("EH-oh-streh"): Goddess of springtime, the east, the dawn, and new beginnings. In the old Anglo-Saxon calendar, the month of April (Eostremonaðr) was named for her.

Ettinham ("ET-in-ham"): The realm or world to the east of Middle Earth, beyond the sunrise. The Ettins, or giants, are primal, alien beings who can often be dangerous and destructive.

Ewemeolc ("YOO-meolk"): A holy tide observed in early February. Ewemeolc celebrates the beginning of spring.

Fetch: A part of the soul that might be thought of as one's guardian spirit. The fetch usually takes on the appearance of an animal.

Fréo ("FRAY-oh"): Goddess of abundance, prosperity, passion, and magic. Sister of Ing Fréa. Fréo is one of the very few Wans (see *Wanham*) who takes an active interest in the events that unfold in Middle Earth. Her name means "lady."

Frige ("FREE-yeh"): Goddess of the household, wisdom, marriage, and childbirth. Woden's consort. She gives her name, which means "beloved," to the sixth day of the week, Friday (Frigesdaeg).

Futhorc ("FOO-thork"): The runes described in the Anglo-Saxon Rune Poem. There are twenty-nine runes addressed in this poem, including all those of the Elder Futhark plus five others, *ac*, *æsc*, *yr*, *ior*, and *ear*.

Fyrn Sidu ("feurn SEE-du"): Pagan Saxon religion. In Old English, this simply means "the old ways."

Galdorcræft ("GALD-or-craft"): The art of working magic through the use of vocalization. Literally, "sound-skill."

Gearde ("YAIRD-eh"): Goddess of the cultivated field. Gearde is an Ettin, but her beauty captured the heart of Ing Fréa, who took her for his bride.

Gesith ("YES-sith"): An oathed member of an inhíred or other Saxon group. A companion or peer.

Gesithscipe ("YES-sith-ship-eh"): The oathed members of a Saxon inhíred. This word literally means "fellowship" or "society."

Glory of Elves: A reference to Sunne, goddess of the sun.

Hallows: A holy tide observed at the end of October, celebrating the beginning of winter.

Hama ("HAHM-ah"): A god who protects the realm of Osgeard from intrusion. Known to the Norse as Heimdall.

Harvest Home: Today most often observed at the autumn
equinox, this holy tide traditionally occurred whenever
the last of the year's crops had been gathered.

Hel: Both the realm of the dead and the name of the Ettin-
goddess who rules over it. Hel's realm is beneath the
world of Dwarfhame. Within the borders of this domain are found the halls of the ancestors.

Hertha ("HERTH-ah"): The earth mother, also known as
Hretha or Eorthe. In the old Anglo-Saxon calendar, the
month of March (Hreðmonað) was named for her.

Híredcniht ("HEAR-ed-k-night"): The child of a gesith.

Híredmann ("HEAR-ed-man"): Any member of an inhíred,
including but not limited to the gesithscipe.

Húsel ("HOO-sel"): A ritual or ceremony in which Saxon Pagans give an offering to their gods, their ancestors, or the
elves. *Húsel* literally means "a sacrifice." The plural is
húsles.

Ides ("EE-des"): A female ancestral spirit. The Saxon Pagan
believes that some mothers continue to watch over their
descendants for many generations. In Old English poetry,
ides was used to honor mortal women, much as contemporary poets and songwriters might employ the word
goddess. The plural is *idesa* ("EE-dess-ah").

Ing Fréa ("Ing FRAY-eh"): God of peace, growth, and fertility. Brother of the beautiful Fréo, and husband of
Gearde. Ing Fréa is the Lord of the Elves. Like his sister,

Ing is one of the Wans (see *Wanham*) who takes an active interest in Middle Earth. *Fréa* is an Old English word for "lord," and thus his name means Lord Ing.

Inhíred ("in-HEAR-ed"): A Saxon family or tribe. This is the term I use, but other words—*mót, hearth, kindred,* and so on—are sometimes used. The structure (or lack thereof) can vary greatly from one group to another. The Saxon tradition strongly encourages group participation. The plural is *inhírdas*.

Lammas ("LAHM-mas"): A holy tide observed in late July or early August. Lammas is the "feast of first fruits," and celebrates the beginning of the autumn harvest season.

Litha ("LEE-tha"): The summer solstice; the point when the daylight hours begin to wane. This holy tide is traditionally celebrated with bonfires.

Mare ("MAR-eh"): A spirit that harms or harasses people in their sleep. The plural is *maran*.

May Day: A holy tide observed on or near the first day of May, celebrating the beginning of summer.

Mægen: A part of the soul that might be thought of as one's spiritual strength. Pronounced like the word *Mayan*.

Middle Earth: Our own world, the physical world. So-called because of its central location between the other worlds or planes of existence.

Mód ("mode"): A part of the soul that maintains one's self-identity. This word evolved into the Modern English word *mood*, meaning a state of mind or emotion. The plural is *módes*.

Módraniht ("MODE-dreh-night"): The first night of Yule, observed on the winter solstice by giving offerings to the *idesa*.

Mona ("MOAN-eh"): The moon god. He gives his name to the second day of the week, Monday (Monnandaeg).

Myne ("MU-neh"): The part of the soul that includes our memories.

Namian ("NAHM-ee-an"): An Old English word meaning "to give a name to." The Namian ceremony is the first rite of passage for Saxon children, in which they are presented to the community and formally given their names.

Orc: Any potentially hostile or dangerous spirit of the dead. Derived from the name Orcus, a Romano-British god of the underworld.

Orlay ("ORE-lay"): All of the actions and words that have shaped who a person is. From the Old English word *orlæg*, often translated as "fate." The source of one's personal wyrd.

Osgeard ("OS-yaird"): The heavenly realm of the Oses, a family of spirits that includes most of the Anglo-Saxon gods and goddesses. Osgeard is found above the world of Elfhame.

Púca ("POOH-ka"): Any mischievous, troublesome spirit. The plural is *púcan*.

Récelsfæt ("RAY-kels-fat"): Any heat-resistant bowl or container used to contain burning incense. Other burnable offerings are also sometimes placed in the récelsfæt.

Rúncræft ("ROON-craft"): The art of using runes, particularly those of the Futhorc, for divination and magic.

Scop ("shope"): A híredmann who entertains during or after a húsel with songs or poetry. The Saxon equivalent of a bard.

Seaxneat ("SAY-ax-nay-at"): A god about whom little is known today. On the continent, he was one of three Saxon gods—along with Woden and Thunor—who were specifically renounced in a formulaic ninth-century Christian baptismal vow.

Sunne ("SOON-eh"): The sun goddess. She gives her name to the first day of the week, Sunday (Sunnandaeg).

Thegn ("thane"): A híredmann who routinely assists the ealdor in some way, and is recognized for doing so. The word literally means "attendant."

Thew ("thyoo"): A custom or way of conducting oneself. Thews might be thought of as tribal morals. The distinction is that a moral is presumed to be universal. Saxon Pagans, being polytheists, recognize that other peoples may and often do play by other rules. Because of a shared set of values, there are some thews that the majority of Saxon Pagans adhere to, but other customs vary from one group to another.

Thunor ("THOO-nor"): God of protection, strength, fertility, and thunder. Son of Woden. He gives his name to the fifth day of the week, Thursday (Thunresdaeg).

Thyle ("THU-leh"): An Old English word meaning "speaker" or "spokesman." Thyle is often an alternate name for the ealdor.

Thyrs ("thoors"): Sometimes called "giants," they are not the same as Ettins. Thyrses are primal, universally destructive powers. They should never be worshipped or revered in any way. These entities are usually confined to the outer realms of fire and ice, but they can occasionally make their way into our plane of existence. In the epic tale of *Beowulf,* the monster Grendel is a thyrs (line 426).

Tiw ("tyoo"): God of justice, oaths, community, and honor. Sometimes considered the Sky Father, he is associated specifically with the North Star. He gives his name to the third day of the week, Tuesday (Tiwesdaeg).

Walhall ("WAHL-hall"): Woden's hall or stead in the heavenly world of Osgeard. Known to the Norse as Valhalla.

Wanham ("WAHN-ham"): The realm or world to the west of Middle Earth, beyond the sunset. The Wans are primal entities. Most take little, if any, interest in mortal affairs.

Wéoh ("WAY-och," ending with a glottal catch, as in *loch*): An image, usually of an Anglo-Saxon god or goddess.

Wéofod ("WAY-oh-fod"): The Saxon altar. Literally, the place where the wéoh stands.

Wéofodthegn ("WAY-oh-fod-thane"): This word translates loosely as "priest," and literally refers to the person who attends and maintains the place where an image of a deity stands.

Wiccecræft ("WEECH-eh-craft"): The skill or art of the witch. Although the surviving early English lore—all of it written down by Christian scribes—makes no clear distinction between wiccecræft and drýcræft, we may surmise from the nature and usage of these words that the former was a simpler, more informal practice.

Woden ("WOE-den"): God of inspiration, fury, healing, and magic. Frige's consort. He wanders among the Seven Worlds, gathering wisdom through his travels. Woden gives his name to the fourth day of the week, Wednesday (Wodnesdaeg).

Wyrd ("weurd"): Often defined loosely as "fate," wyrd is the process in which the future unfolds from our orlay. Since all things are connected, wyrd is sometimes viewed as a vast, infinite web expressing this connectivity.

Yule: A seasonal midwinter celebration, beginning on Módraniht (the night of the winter solstice) and continuing for twelve or more days.

Bibliography

Bates, Brian. *The Real Middle Earth*. New York: Palgrave MacMillan, 2002.

Branston, Brian. *The Lost Gods of England*. London: Constable and Company, 1957.

Buckland, Raymond. *Practical Candleburning Rituals*. St. Paul, MN: Llewellyn, 1970.

Crossley-Holland, Kevin. *The Norse Myths*. New York: Pantheon Books, 1980.

Davidson, H. R. Ellis. *Gods and Myths of Northern Europe*. Harmondsworth, UK: Penguin Books, 1964.

Donaldson, Talbot E., trans. *Beowulf*. New York: W. W. Norton, 1975.

Fee, Christopher R. *Gods, Heroes, and Kings: The Battle for Mythic Britain*. Oxford, UK: Oxford University Press, 2001.

Greer, John Michael. *A World Full of Gods: An Inquiry into Polytheism*. Tucson, AZ: ADF Publishing, 2005.

Griffiths, Bill. *Aspects of Anglo-Saxon Magic*. Norfolk, UK: Anglo-Saxon Books, 1996.

Harrison, Michael. *The Roots of Witchcraft*. Secaucus, NJ: Citadel Press, 1974.

Hartley, Dorothy. *Lost Country Life*. New York: Pantheon Books, 1979.

Herbert, Kathleen. *Looking for the Lost Gods of England*. Norfolk, UK: Anglo-Saxon Books, 1994.

Hutton, Ronald. *The Pagan Religions of the Ancient British Isles: Their Nature and Legacy*. Malden, MA: Blackwell Publishing, 1991.

Jennings, Pete. *The Northern Tradition*. Somerset, UK: Capall Bann Publishing, 2003.

Jones, Prudence, and Nigel Pennick. *A History of Pagan Europe*. New York: Barnes & Noble Books, 1995.

Krasskova, Galina. *Exploring the Northern Tradition: A Guide to the Gods, Lore, Rites, and Celebrations from the Norse, German, and Anglo-Saxon Traditions*. Franklin Lakes, NJ: New Page Books, 2005.

Laing, Lloyd, and Jennifer Laing. *Anglo-Saxon England*. New York: Charles Scribner's Sons, 1979.

Matthews, John. *Robin Hood: Green Lord of the Wildwood*. Glastonbury, UK: Gothic Image Publications, 1993.

Schramm, Ken. *The Compleat Meadmaker*. Boulder, CO: Brewers Publications, 2003.

Simpson, Jacqueline, and Steve Roud. *A Dictionary of English Folklore*. Oxford, UK: Oxford University Press, 2000.

Thorsson, Edred. *Witchdom of the True*. Smithville, TX: Runa-Raven Press, 1999.

Whitelock, Dorothy. *The Beginnings of English Society*. Harmondsworth, UK: Penguin Books, 1977.

To Write to the Author

If you wish to contact the author or would like more information about this book, please write to the author in care of Llewellyn Worldwide and we will forward your request. Both the author and publisher appreciate hearing from you and learning of your enjoyment of this book and how it has helped you. Llewellyn Worldwide cannot guarantee that every letter written to the author can be answered, but all will be forwarded. Please write to:

Alaric Albertsson
c/o Llewellyn Worldwide
2143 Wooddale Drive, Dept. 978-0-7387-1536-0
Woodbury, Minnesota 55125-2989, U.S.A.

Please enclose a self-addressed stamped envelope for reply, or $1.00 to cover costs. If outside U.S.A., enclose international postal reply coupon.

Many of Llewellyn's authors have websites with additional information and resources. For more information, please visit our website at http://www.llewellyn.com